Life and the Fields

Life and the Fields

New and Selected Poems by

George Keithley

Turning Point Books

Published by Turning Point
P.O. Box 541106
Cincinnati, OH 45254-1106

ISBN: 9781625492968

Poetry Editor: Kevin Walzer
Business Editor: Lori Jareo

Visit us on the web at www.turningpointbooks.com.

Also by George Keithley

Poetry
Night's Body
The Starry Messenger
The Midnight Train
Living Again
Earth's Eye
The Burning Bear
To Bring Spring
Scenes from Childhood
Song in a Strange Land
The Donner Party

Fiction
Ring of Fire
Flesh and Dust

Drama
The Best Blood of the Country

Literary Journalism
Themes in American Literature, Coeditor

For Carol

Contents

Life and the Fields

From me to thee glad serenades,
Dances for thee I propose saluting thee, adornments
    and feastings for thee,
        And the sights of the open landscape and the high-
        spread sky are fitting,
And life and the fields, and the huge and thoughtful
    night.

—Walt Whitman

NEW

AND UNCOLLECTED POEMS

Voices, Stillness

Late on a clear night
along the Missouri
the last of our fire

flickers into blue
or blood-red

embers. They shudder,
shift—break

open. Sparks
flare up

forming their thin
swarm. But fall back

into this world.
The embers settle,

hiss with fierce
persistent life.

We listen to
the rhythmic lapping

of the water. We
hear its current,

almost the sound
of voices singing

on the far shore
until they drift off

like the first souls
to cut timber for

the fishing camp.
Who sank pilings

to support their pier
and built the flood—

blasted boathouse.
Peaked roof, pinewood

walls and floor washed
away. Where the pier

collapsed the current
sloshes each pair

of skeletal pilings.
Now it pours down—

now it pours down
everywhere—this

deepening stillness
while the full moon

climbs the sky—
While it rises over

our dusky embers.

The ruins, the dark
And glistering river.

Building a Fire

Wind thrashes the trees. At the near
edge of the clearing the camp dogs
cower, won't approach. Though the guide
changed his shirt his boots reek of blood.

Stooping beneath the trees, rising,
circling with a close, level stride,

women collect the deadfall—all
of it—armfuls bristling, brittle.

Two walking together bring in
three limbs, stout, shattered, for the axe.

In the hour when the wind is down
at last, before the coming dark,

they construct the tinder pile, boughs
broken to size, latticed. Each tier

settled across its broader base,
skeletal, unlike a house. Now

they lay the fresh-cut logs over
the kindling. Night is falling when
their work, woven of wood and air,
is touched with a fluttering torch.

Lines at 2 a.m. on the Sea of Cortez

The bright morning brought its mirage—
the far shore and one shadow-free
inlet loomed before us. Until
two gulls swooped across our deckhouse.
That pair rising with a single shriek
into the sudden overcast.
Then it was dusk all day. Humid,
warm, the sullen light of a low sky.

When evening arrived without stars
we saw the vast gulf grow formless—
Brackish tide pools, coves, a pocked reef

and each white beach slipped out of sight
with the sea snakes. Old turtles, all
but blind, cleaving dense clouds of silt.

The swarming crabs, hammer-head sharks,
swordfish, prowling rays. The nearly
level sea itself invisible . . .

Our boat bobs among shallow troughs,
horse-like, irritable before
the worst weather. In water quiet
but not at rest—the sleepless stir
of a tense calm. Now blue-black clouds
quake with storm light and we know
this night has a life of its own,
we hear it breathing in the dark.

Iron, Old Tin, & Wood

Bean fields, corn fields, they lose their green luster.
Twilight dims and fills
the stillness before a storm.
I'm tired of driving but I don't want supper.
Outside of town I pull the car over—
A giant heap of scrap metal sprawls above the river.

Late at night by the riverbed
the odor of iron, old tin, and wood.

My wife and daughters sleep two thousand miles
away. I wonder if they think of me in the dark?
If they forget my face and my voice?
If I could find them the way the aging tin
finds me alone in the night with its sharp tang?

After dark rain
birds sing in the rusty dawn—
I hear them in another life.

Lying here, I've been dreaming of coming home.
I wake up and my arms are stretched out
to this one, to each one, at the same time.
This is how rain reaches through the night
to wake the grass. Then the birds come to sing.

In Wind and Rain

Crossing the high meadow above Wolf River
the wind deepens the waves of tall grass
bowing beneath it. Two blackbirds startled
into flight complain *zeeer! zeeer!* Magpies row
over the sweet clover and the day glows
as it darkens. A fresh scent fills the air.
When rain arrives the pelting drops rattle
each patch of dry nettles. A searching rain
takes the shape of everything it touches:
nests, nettles, weathered outcrop, seething
grass. The wind sweeps headlong down to the brim
of the meadow where a footpath glimmers,
already mud-slick, sluiced by onrushing
rain. At dusk the wind stalls, hovers. Withholds
itself. Gathering not time, which it scatters,
but eternity in a storm of leaves—
the one large-limbed tree towering over
the fence, the black iron gate flung open
to our hillside cemetery. The gale grasps,
wrenches loose, tilts, uproots the ancient
memorial elm. It lays the quivering
canopy, crushed boughs, and that great trunk,
its rough-ridged bark black with wet, prone
among the graves. All night scouring white pine
crosses, stone tablets, urns, rainwater pools
then welters. Once the run-off starts the elm
plummets the slope, plunging into Wolf River,
its turbulent current rushing downstream
with the low urgent roaring that persists
in wind and rain. Together now they drive
the river. Writhing, churning, it never rests.

Early Morning In November

You woke to this inward silence
and song that seek each other
without words—

No sound of your neighbor's axe
in the wet woods.

Shivering you hike across
a swale of coarse grass.

Here beside the shore
where a willow's

leaves turn
blue-brown

before falling
a chill light

shelters in
the lean branches.

In the mist over the lake
one black-billed swan
whistles to another.

The Gospel According to Thomas

He says if we discover the meaning
of these words when we die
He will watch us as we fall asleep
and touch his hand to my mouth
and yours and we will not taste death.

He says if we were meant to rise
into heaven when we die
then we would arrive long after the birds
who are familiar with wandering in the air
and they would overshadow us by far.

He says if we were meant to sink
into the sea when we die
we would float among the fish
who are already happy in their home
and we would envy how easily they swim.

He says we are not to wonder how
it will be when we die
but see the way stones and trees are born;
then if we want to appear wise
we ought to ask a child of seven days.

He says if we will leave the world
nothing when we die
in poverty the angels who open
the tombs will laugh when they arrive;
there is no gold in a good man's grave.

He says we won't see the separate sex
of one another when we die.
Male or female we return
to our origin and begin to heal—

which is the nature of the soul.

He says, therefore, to go naked
not only when we die
but here today; if we will drop our clothes
in the dirt and trample them the way children do
then we will see Him come uncovered too.

A Valley Oak in Early Spring

In the blue twilight
of the open woods

this corpse of raw wrists
whose bones are sticks

this blood brother
of birds and stones

listens to the pulse
in its limbs

a quiet voice
singing above the slim

apron of pollen scum
on the round pond's rim.

The Angel of Solitude

At daybreak I knelt by the shallows.
    Ripples nudged the skiff—pine green
        paint worn thin from knocking

against our pier. One dead
    loon drifted ashore
        overnight—we'll bury

the remains this morning.
    You're here, spirit, silent
        as ever while you gather

to yourself the shrill squall
    of the young gull wading out
        from the sedge grass. High-

stepping over a broken oar-
    lock, driftwood, damp stones.
        He quiets now. Moves on

as I walk onto the pier. Minnows
    dart, disappear among cedar
        pilings sunk into bedrock

of the spring-fed lake. Its deep
    current flowing through
        finger-long fronds, tendrils.

In that dim filtered light lie
    cloud-colored bones delicate
        as feathers. Hunters' shell

casings. Once the gull reaches
     mid-water he perches
          on the buoy bobbing

in a low wind. The world
     within and his own quick
          nature—each alone in

the heart of the other.
     Few waves. Out there the purr,
          or plash, of slow-rocking

water. Until the disturbance
     starts with a sudden swell.
          A familiar motion—felt

before it's seen—like this
     intake of breath across
          the lake to the stone beach,

the pier. Is it once more
     the angel of solitude
          departing? Or the lone

gull aloft now—rowing
     toward a quarter moon
          low in the morning sky?

THE DONNER PARTY

Taking the Trail

I am George Donner a dirt farmer
who left the snowy fields
around Springfield, Illinois
in the fullness of my life

and abandoned the land
where we had been successful
and prosperous people

and brought a party of eighty men
women and children
west by wagon.

For weeks my wife Tamsen
was the talk of women
meeting in the marketplace

keeping warm indoors
pricing yards of dry goods
and rolls of ribbon

while we laid up large stores
for our journey
across the unsettled country.

But the last pools of ice
had disappeared from the road
when we set out.

This was during the damp days
of early April when the trees shake
off their snow

in orchard and wood
and begin to bud.
That winter we'd read reports

on California climate where the soil is sewn
with streams in every season.
All year you smell the bloom in the air

and farm that fertile land in the yellow valley heat.
So we prepared to go,
packing our pewter and plates.

Carefully we chose our daughters' clothes.
Their winter coats and woolen leggings
we laid in a trunk lifted by two ebony handles.

Tamsen sorted her silks
and bolts of bright cloth, cambric and calico,
and much more plain muslin.

With the wagons drawn onto the lawn and loaded
I assured her, "Once we're there, dear,
we'll know the worth of all our work."

As the oxen swelled ahead in their harness
my family led the line of nine wagons at the start.
Six were filled with freight.

My wife held our infant daughter Frances on her lap;
Eliza, six years old, and Georgia, four,
were seated on the floor.

My brother Jacob joined us
with his wife Elizabeth
and their three dutiful boys.

And our friends the family of James Reed
who made money in mines
and rails and carpentry

and drove a huge house-wagon
equipped with passenger door
and collapsible stairs—

A portable stove.
A braided rug on the floor.
A table and chairs.

With Reed in the rear we followed
the fat flanks of our cattle across familiar fields
until the green skin of the Sangamon River could be seen
sunning itself like a lazy snake.

The Platte River and the Prairie

Buffalo bathed in the brown river
widening the water
while half the herd went on
feeding in a field.

It was a warm June morning,
even the boys on sentry duty
sat on the bank watching

dung colored cows wallow in the water
flowing around their flanks
so we weren't prepared

when the young Pawnee
on pony and on foot
crept quietly into camp.

Some wore paint smeared down their cheeks.
All had taken care to shave
the whole head except a scalp-lock,

a single shock of hair on top of the skull
to which they tied a thatch of hair
thinned from the tail of a deer,

then dyed blood-red. Every brave
had brought his rifle and appeared
eager to prove his skill—

We waded into a tall patch of prairie grass
to see them shoot.
One by one as they knelt down

each man put on a wolf skin,
a complete pelt from head to tail
long enough to cover

his nakedness as he bent over.
Almost at once the hunter acquired
a queer kind of innocence:

He became a creature more natural.
As if he'd lost the gift of reason
and in its absence

he looked a little less stiff, more graceful,
surely, than the rest of us;
moving with the agility of an animal

allowed to follow its feelings.
However, his lower legs were exposed,
as were his hands, reaching out, undeniably human.

The head of the wolf hid the bald
skull of the man inside.
Under its jaws his eyes glowed.

This was the disguise the stalker wore
to make the buffalo ignore him;
he was no more than a wolf

come to clean the carcass of a dead cow...
Men filled their rifles now. And fell
to all fours, crawling away in the waving grass.

While the sun beat down on us
the buffalo bent eating the green wind
in which their faces disappeared.

The wolf-men on their hands and knees
approached the herd and not one was seen.
When they shot a big cow our children cheered!

*

Then one morning we left the river
far behind us and a small bird flew
round and round, flirting in the field.

We loafed out in a lazy line and heard
the meadowlark's song,
tsee-oo, tsee-air, all day long.

*

Late one day we stopped
where a grove of ash trees gripped the wall
of a sunken slough.

Parties passing this way
had watered at Ash Hollow
and left it looking like a swamp.

The marsh was marked by cattle tracks;
spears of grass trampled in the mud.
The trail to the water was slick as grease.

We backed down, sliding our wagons down
the slope a few feet at a time.
Drivers had to drag the cattle.

I waited while our stock
started to drink
and then I walked off with my wife.

Hand in hand we went
up the slope to lie
beneath the trees.

The sun no longer burned
the sky, and we had seen
the hills grow more severe.

But it was still gentle
green country like the kind
we came from,

a patchwork prairie
broken by woods and farms
where we made our homes,

and more than happy
to find ourselves alone
at last we turned
into each other's arms.

Ash Hollow

Your green eyes
seeing the hollow
sinking in the shade
grow dim—

Time let me
lay with you a long
time let me

play with your hair
around my hand
your warm

tongue lag, linger
or slide slow
time let me

go and race
a fair race my
legs against yours

ash leaves vanish
off the cool rise
the sky

and the wide hills
draw down night
on this high place
and your green eyes.

Cutting a Trail

Two weeks breaking brush in the canyons
hopping across
a web of creeks.

Down in the narrows
men had to chop with axes and picks
through thickets of willows and wild rose.

Breen bitched about his back and mine hurt too.
"I'd rather keep up
than stop to eat in the shade.

If I quit," he said, "the pain splits
my spine
like a blade."

However we did stand
admiring the terrain
while the women rinsed our shirts.

In a trance Jacob's oldest son
let the sweat run
from his blond beard. Left

his hand on the haft of his axe.
He stared up the slope where he was to cut
but his mind was gone—

A man may see a valley
overgrown with trees
a stream struck by sunlight

and in the cave of his chest
his heart falls

because he loves

the land too much with his eyes.
He is jealous
of the generous nature of all things

vegetable or mineral
and the wild life
and the long lights of space

so he cannot move
on, nor come
deep into that place.

Land Logic

We crept beneath our quilts at Pilot Peak.
I tossed all night, badgered by our bad luck.
I prayed we had seen the end of it. But no...

We woke to find the Peak was wrapped in snow!
Its dome wore a cap of fresh fallen snow.
Its flanks were wrinkled with crisp white creases.

I saw the dismay in many faces
and heard the fatigue in my friends' voices.
The advent of autumn was an unhappy omen...

We were weeks from California, and someone
must travel to Sutter's settlement
on the Sacramento River and ride back

with provisions. Flour and dried meat. On pack
horses or mules. "My wife's a sparrow,
she has no hips," I said, "she has no shadow."

Ladies laughed at this. I added, "And we know
our little ones are too weak go on
eating like lizards." I spoke at midday

as the sun crossed over us and dried away
a fine-spun frost...Stanton and McCutchen
on plodding mounts set out for Sutter's place.

The sun scorched the sky and still a trace
of snow remained upon the peak. We kept
our cattle grazing by a running pool.

A week passed, the water every day was cool
and clean. On most mornings the sun seemed slow

to warm, the grass looked glossy with moisture.

We wanted only to rest, at this juncture.
Seeing the snow, no one wished to look back
on our bad luck or talk of it anymore.

Reflection only led us to deplore
the sudden end of summer and lament
the time we wasted in this trap. Whole days

spent unloading. Stupid disputes. Delays
caused by the cattle roaming or Hastings' wrong
advice... We were warned that to survive

we must lay up grass and water for a dry drive
of two days. Which meant at worst we might
travel a day and a night—where we instead

wandered a week in the desert and left dead
a third of our herd of cattle. Add a third
of the wagons abandoned, still it doesn't explain

all the destruction done. We could never regain
the time taken, nor our goods or livestock left
on the salt. But this was not the only cost.

There is a land logic which we lost . . .
A sense of the likelihood of new terrain
to sustain us. The same logic that lives

in our blood, telling us that bottomland gives
promise for planting. Or for example,
the simple certainty that we would find

spring water among rocks when the sun reclined
on green slopes gleaming like good pasture.

But we hurried out only to discover

a prickly patch of greasewood growing over
the dry soil, white with alkali...
Nothing in nature was what it might seem!

The promise of finding forage beside a stream
proved false as well—both banks were bare
although the current there cut swift and deep.

We lost the last advantage which could keep
our company from harm. It was this sense
of the land that had departed in a dream
while we went on like souls that are still asleep.

The Division of Day and Night

Crossing a flat valley at our level pace
eighteen wagons travel
fifteen miles daily.
Each crossing brings our teams

to fresh grass by the springs.
In a meadow mountain sheep
crop the grass.

Antelope keep to the high brown slope.
A long tiring climb
down from the hunt—

Hear the children singing?
Now, at mealtime,
roasting meat begins to smoke.

Dusk arrives
dragging the cold across those rocks
above us.

Three weeks into September
leaves change color,
clutter the grass.

In our *Almanac* this date marks
the sun and moon brought in balance—
The autumn equinox.

Aspen lose their leaves. Stand
bone-white while the heavens
divide the hours, day and night.

The sun displays the earth or stars

barely illuminate the sky
while we who inhabit the land
go equally in dark and light.

When Our Children Were Asleep

When our children were asleep
Tamsen took my hand
and dressed the wound
with a clean cloth

while I held my breath.
The pain was swelling
far up my arm.

She opened her blouse.
"Look at this,"
she whispered.

"You can count my ribs—
Feel here and press
your fingers in."

She unpinned her hair
and shook it out
so the auburn braids

dropped down her spine
and seemed to steam
against her skin.

When she turned her breasts
were pale and cool
as wax. She whispered,

"Look how my hips
hardly hold a skirt
in place anymore."

As I joined her
in the blanket
on the pine floor

with pleasure
she remarked upon the slack skin
that flapped on my legs.

"Surely," I told her,
"yours are more
firm. And shapely."

She laughed lying
in my arms,
my hand at rest
on her small waist.

A Death-Bed Confession

Our fire glistened on his face.

When his lips moved I bowed my head to listen.
"I helped to kill her husband," he confessed.
"That day we dropped behind the others?

His wife rode ahead with yours—
On the Humboldt River, me and Spitzer,
we jumped Wolfinger.

I wrapped my belt
around his throat
and fired one shot.

I cut his moneybelt,
Spitzer lifted his watch,
we split his gold.

We laid his corpse across his horse.
We rode off half a mile—
Hid him in the brush behind a little hill."

At length Reinhardt grew calm.
A coma left him in a listless state.
When he relaxed his legs ceased to shake.

Before the widow woke up he had died.
We dug a shallow grave near the creek,
not striking solid mud beneath the snow.

Soft snow which we smacked down with a spade.
Then we crawled back inside.
Later we had to steal out at night.

We dug him up to remove the necessary meat.
Arms and legs at the start.
Then the heart and liver as well.

We would not have done this
but it was so long since anyone had eaten
a meal.

When we returned to the hut my wife was weeping.
I told her, "He paid for his crime with his life.
If we share his corpse he may save someone else."

Some nights the air froze
our tracks and
preserved the prints

where our boots sank
into the drifts
going to the graves,

but these were buried
when the wind arose
shrouding the creek

blowing oblivion over
low shrubs
and snapping the aspens.

So we ate
and went to bed at night
and awoke in the morning

seeing the surrounding mountains grow
remote and insignificant
the vague slopes

never dissolved
but disappearing
day by day in the omnivorous wind.

Even the large pines that stand
like landmarks here in the meadow
were lost in the easy lambence of the snow.

The only permanence is in our past
where the prairie withdraws while winter forms
its wide quiet with so little color
that the covered shapes feel familiar.

After This Life We Will Listen

Our last days are like the first

mild morning
which arrives in April—
Almost any noise is a surprise.

Squirrels race around the roof
scratching the thatchwork boughs.
They tumble down the dark walls,

they leave us and leap onto the trees
where the birds shriek and sing.
One morning we hear the alders rustle

in the incessant rain.
Later the sun slips over the meadow.
Blue jays dive

in long dips
flashing from shadow to shadow
while an enormous chorus fills the air.

After this life we will listen,
lying in the loose grains of dirt
with our eyes sealed shut against the roots

that reach for them; we will hear
our breath begin again, the engine of the brain
begin humming in the mulch, and we will climb

with our nails, and teeth, biting through the black earth,
clawing away the soil, hand and mouth
tearing out of our wet tombs forever to find

it is Spring! The grass
is wet, waving toward the trees.
Their bark is yellow or brown and the underside of the leaves

is so gentle
we are afraid
to touch it.

Come into a meadow where the crystal snow-
crust shrinks under
the shade of the rocks...

After this life we will listen
to the judgments of bears and the deer
awaking.

The birds over the treetops crossing and calling
in the long leaves.
The red eyes of berries

surprise us. And the deer
and the fox who know we are here
on the brink of the meadow—

they smell our fear
floating into the grass like a shallow river
establishing its edges.

They find us and follow the cool water
from the mountains, their eyes bring the blue light
of evening onto the valley,

the prairie almost lost, drowning in darkness,
sparks of stars already spinning
downstream, traveling in the tall weeds.

After this life we will listen
to the long river running through the soil
saying it is Spring—

the sun has begun to burn
the brown needles nesting on the ground
around our graves.

Jays perch in the pines and cry
and wherever we may sleep
among the dead we will rise

together under the trees
like men who are set free
from the folly of a dream

into the fragrant morning
to hear the heavy stream
of our blood begin to sing,

our souls awake and warm once more
and weaving like a fire
when the light begins to dance
in the land of our desire.

SONG IN A STRANGE LAND

I shall vanish and be no more,
but the land over which I now roam
shall remain
and change not..

—Omaha Indian warrior song

Lincoln in Love

When we hear the song
of two tanagers
and stand in the warm
shade of an elm
I recall this dream—
It was night; yet
the yellowthroats,
too, were out. We
said nothing. Heard
one bird calling,
one bird answering.
But by daylight
whatever they sing
is a mystery. Lost
in my long ears.

Might we believe,
ever, their serenade?
Or do they enjoy
the chagrin of children
like us? They must
cherish the anguish
of adults as much—

Huge hands falling
open, eyes, stinging,
a man paces back
and forth, explaining
his marriage to
the darkness where
his dog sits silent,
the mule waits to
eat. Our feet wade
the field of natural law

submerged in sucking
mud and it seems
we must stop and
sink at any hour
because we are weak
and the only peace
is in our sleep
and the only power
is in our dreams.

A Photo by Brady

His large faith looks like ours for he believes
like us that his camera's report
records nature. The silent lives
of men are filmed where they were flung out
in the sunny grass. Here the scene achieves
simplicity. For its flat calm distorts
our field of vision as though the men's
mouths made no more noise below his lens.

On the grey grass or the sky nothing flies
from fear. There's some withdrawal
of smoke, a haze beneath the trees
where the surprised troops fall along the hill.
Each figure rests in an insane ease—
all conscious grace, all that is natural,
halted as sunlight floods the aperture.
Heavy flank fire floats in the air.

Wedged against the trees—there—a white
church bleaches the hilltop. With pure
release men sprawl in the grass, prostrate,
their shirts blown open on the pasture.
The long sense of balance is accurate
and quiet. The thoughtless weight of leisure
on their legs and groin and arms as the church-ground
takes the sun and their pale breasts burn unbound.

After Antietam

The breeze rises
loud off the crisp grass—
The lame in the field scream prayers, and wait
for the bearers. The kindly, the careful. Arriving now.
The deserters crawl through the long grass.

Upstream, McClellan's pursuit hesitates.
His delay, his bloodless pause, spares
Hood's hard-marched, bone-lean forces. And Lee's.
Like rumor, the ghosts of these troop off south.
Rewarded with whiskey
Colonel Ferrero's thirsty 51sts drink happily.
Lie close to me…
By the Dunker church in the smoking grove.
Autumn in the mauve wood
the farm girls will rein in
 and sit their mounts silent…
The ponies lap and blow at the shallow stream.
Sunny hills swell.
A detail slips through the ripe corn
fetching shattered horses.
In pens the swine are full for the harvest
butchering and the temperate feasts.
These wait, and again all wait.

My love, lie in the day with me, into the shade
and hour of a sane order. When flesh and flesh
breed history, word of the act: Rodman slain,
his men safe, dry. Burnside baffled.
Cautious McClellan, wary and loving
the men walking in at dusk from the blue copse.
Their dragging, piling motion orderly
clearing cornfield and hayfield of the carcasses
of cavalry-, wheel-, and pack-horses,

arranging memory on the green valley.
Late September down the valley
the wind smolders the sweet greasy smoke
of the torched horses,
the wind black, the gristle popping.

Arm in arm, my love, lie on with me
as the gusty November snow settles
uneasy against the scattered nettles,
across the black hay, the scorched timothy.
Silent as dormant limbs, as the season
freezes, north into Pennsylvania's hills;
at thaw the seed distending in the soil
sprouts rapid pasture, green to a weak sun!
Out of May the copper stream rills under
the fume of lilac blooming, the arched stone
bridge. The stand of poplar saplings rises
to the oriole. Into the summer
leaning warm, lie on with me, my love, low
springs the wind, tall grow the raving grasses.

He Is Burning

He is burning
to see her, his eyes
are smeared with smoke.
The flame in his flesh

a torchlight which leads
the man home. Four days
on horse from the hunting camp,
the huts hung with skins—

unlike those long houses
built of elm bark
in the village where she sleeps
among so many women.

At night now he sees
the meadow of her brown eyes,
her breasts blossom
above the bent grass—

He is burning to hold her
close the way the wind
holds fire in a bush
until it eats down to the dirt.

At dawn he hears
the whole town waking—
a dozen or
more dogs barking—

Barking at the dawn!
Rides in to find the fields
wild with horses, his hogs
driven from their pen.

The lodges are lit like kindling
for cooking. Fire consumes
their frames. Walls fly up,
they outleap the flames—

Men white as ice
are chasing the children out
of the village to
mingle among the hogs,

the women wading after
in a surf of skirts
and grass, struck
across the back with sticks—

He is burning
to bury his knife
in the breast of the blond lieutenant—
The raiding party

withdraws to the fort
above the mouth
of the shrieking river—
Behind them a hundred homes,

walls of black bark,
are blazed to the ground:
"Precaution
against contamination."

Stragglers return from the fields.
While they gather
the wind weaves the hair
of young and old together

as it weaves the braids of water
flowing by their feet—
the river where they see
their faces floating away.

Black Hawk in Hiding

1
Everyone can see me standing in the stockade
built to contain the worst of the white
soldiers: cowards; drunks; those who disobeyed
their officers. Now it houses prisoners
of war. The soldiers grow sober
gawking at us in the sunlight
slipping over the wood-and-wire fence.

2
The chain that binds my wrists pulls hard
beneath my balls—and twists.
From daybreak to dusk it clings to my legs;
like an iron vine it clings.
An iron bar is fastened to both feet
to make certain I won't run far
and I don't try; I stand still.

3
I hope I will die soon. The first morning
I'll wade into the woods around Rock River,
stopping knee-deep among the thatchwork
mesh of creepers. There, under the trees,
I'll breathe the brown bittersweet stink
of stale fish and grass, keeping back
in the wet shade where no one can see me.

How Crazy Horse Was Killed

1
Because there was gold in the Black Hills
people wished to find their fair share and dig it out,
which required a road through the quiet country.
We knew our duty to protect the public:
We kept our eyes open for anyone who incited
trouble among agency Indians or those hostiles
who refused to live on our land when invited.
We had to watch him in particular; we were told
he had such power with his people.
Difficult to understand—
He stood no bigger than a boy,
his hair soft and straw-brown,
his skin no darker than a white's with a tan.
He ruled himself with terrible restraint
and disdained dancing or wearing paint.
So we thought half-breed but he was a full-blood.
Our informants agreed he gained his fame
and influence from visions. He'd seen his horse
prancing in a wild way on the landscape
of the other world. Hence his name.

A schemer. That's certain. What was he planning?
We sent spies—they returned—told
tall tales to guarantee their pay.
Well, we needed someone we could trust.

Regardless of the rumors he was only human.
Why not find him a sweet young woman?
We brought a half-breed girl into the hills
and let him discover her. Let her live
with him. Why not? Once each week
she stole back to the fort to report.
I think you'll agree this procedure

though perhaps treacherous was necessary
or we would never have any peace.

2
She informed us he planned to leave the territory!
We were truly alarmed—
He'd pass among people we were sworn to protect
and no one doubted that he was armed.
(Were we to think he meant to hunt
elk and buffalo with his bare hands?)

We sent a party to request that he visit
the fort and discuss his journey with us.
Troops rode along to escort him. Would you have us
leave him unguarded? It's certain
he knew of the warriors we held in prison—
he'd be watching for his chance to free them
and we would never have any peace.

3
Our cannon were concealed by a wall of cottonwoods.
Where the road approached a river of dust
drifted into the trees as the party proceeded.
He rode into the fort—no trouble until he dismounted.
He wished to speak with the officer in command.

Our plan was to jail him overnight
then hurry him out of the country under arms.
We'd prepared a high walkway to the door
of the guardhouse so he couldn't see it.
Several hundred horse troops, their number increased
by the local Lakota tribal police,
formed a corridor to the jail
but he heard men dragging their chains.
When he saw the low building with its bars
on the windows—he went out of his head.

He dropped his blanket and showed a knife.
Someone bent his arms behind him but he slipped free.

He began slashing at us and his blade drew blood.
So the sentry stuck a bayonet in his back
and our worries were over. He fell gently
face down. We slid him inside and put him to bed
where he died. At sunrise his aged parents arrived
to wrap his body in a buffalo robe. They left him, then,
on a scaffold in the Badlands. Without witness. Unless
there was a prairie hen and her young hunched in a bush.
Overhead the eagle hawks kept looping like patrols.

Outsiders will sympathize with him, of course,
but we had to kill this fool or fight a war
with his friends. Or we could give up our guns,
unlock the gates, let everyone run free,
and we would never have any peace.

The Boxcar

Quietly they stand at the door
of a railroad boxcar
found in a field and
holding only hay now. They both listen before
helping each other
enter. A cemetery
stillness settles upon the prairie.
After the young couple
climb into the car, they stoop to gather
armfuls of straw—enough to make
the modest mattress he shares with her.

His shirt and her dress are their sheet
spread over their stiff bed
of straw. The sun swells,
hanging overhead. Indifferent to the dark heat
about them, they lie
an hour later on the floor
of the boiling boxcar and ignore
the light leaving the pale
prairie. Body and spirit utterly
lost to the summer life of soil
or sky—at rest in the dying day.

A red moon rises from these weeds.
At one edge of the field
a dog emerges
from the dusty shower of stubble or dry seeds
it shakes from its hair.
Walking home, they hear its bark
behind them. The moon bays in the dark
as they return to town,
where love lies buried deep in the unclear

souls of men and women waiting
only to lie down, to be born once more.

The Great Northern Railway

The iron exposed like bone begins to cloud,
going blue in the October cold.

The strands of steel starting from St. Paul
float onto the flatlands,
feeling through the morning frost.

Wind threshes the grass into grains
of golden chaff.

When a black-neck elk wanders out
wearing patches of chaff like snow
melting in the yoke of his mane

no one says a word around the railbed.
He lifts one leg over.

His hoof hits one wood tie,
trying his weight on it
before he'll cross the tracks

as though he has heard something—

The miles of silence saying nothing
is coming

and he decides to wade out
into the cold waves of weeds.

When we turn to go
we take the weather with us

leaving

the veins of coldness
the long iron lines of isolation

plunging into the prairie
and sinking under the grass at last.

Riding Home

Riding home in an open jeep
after practice we lean
into a turn, pull back, hold
ourselves straight on the steel seat.

All this country is cold—
You hear hissing heat
blowing from the brown
box below your knees.

Before the road reaches town
the boy driving sees
a field without fence on one side.
He whips the wheel to his right

and we glide
over gravel shoulder onto the light
surface snow—
the field frozen by the end of fall.

The jeep jumps from furrow to furrow.
Talk of football
or the stories of school girls stop,
riders are flung

onto the stiff farmland where we drop
to our knees. Unharmed among
the frozen rows we find
our footing and shout—

stumbling at nightfall behind
the stalled car. When we walk out
the blood still
in the veins of every voice

rises, of its own will,
and we rejoice—
shouting as though the deep
ground would waken from its grim routine,

the spring soil asleep
in the bed of time, O grave and green.

A Spring Night in Nashville

While we walk along the water our arms wear
the swaying air
warm as if with fever
until we turn from the Cumberland river
down a dim street and climb
to the steam of a single room.

Still the rhythm of the river
provides a pulse that throbs in the corner clubs,
in studios where the gleam of wire guitars
softens the resonance of steel

and in the evening air we feel

all songs built on the beat and tone of loneliness

but your tongue teaches music to my mouth
and our hands hear the singing of our skin.

*

A slow rain scratches the roof
when we crawl to sleep, pulling up a pale sheet.

The mind no longer lingers at the sill of the skull
but walks into the wet woods which shape one side of a hill.

Now another leaves the body in its bed.
With such light step as not to waken man or woman
the soul too steals toward sleep beneath bleak clouds—
halts at the high window, turning to see
ourselves wrapped in one white sheet,
a cumbersome quilt across our legs
as we lie in the falling glow

of our flesh feeling surely
this is the darkness which will shelter us.
This is the night we know, in which we dream of dying,
and we die.

*

Alone the soul strolls in the night
by the full river flowing
below the cemetery of the old South,
a disparity of graves growing low in the grass
and tall tombs where the dead were sealed inside the stones
which prolong the process of their decay.

But the ghost who goes forth from us does not regard
these silver stones in the graveyard
more than a moment—they are not important—
does not lean long looking at the memorial plaques
on public walls, stooping to read an inscription in the street.

Browses before the wet window
of a bookstore and sees the display of bibles;
will not buy these or other books, not maps or poems or
novels.

Perceives a patrol car cruising
the quiet neighborhood all night to note
these few men still on the street, white and black,
who walk like the soul itself without work or rest.

The warehouse guard crouches over his coffee.
His foot bounds on the board floor to that tune
he whistles.
One watchman on the loading dock listens

late to his radio—music floats over the freight yard.

How can the conscience of the night contain
the pain of the human heart rising in room after room?

O even in sleep our blood floods our arms;
its red rhythm stirs our skin
to open like roses, my wrist below your breast.

*

O beautiful black night when we are born
out of the distance dark and unseen
into the stillness of a city
whose streets are songs of longing
which wait for the words of our first breath.

The mind paces the porch of morning
while the spirit passes
over moist soil to its home—

The soul returns to its skin,
flowing within ourselves as the river arrives
out of the east, glowing and gliding—

O love, let us join
in the spring and be one
like the current of the Cumberland, raised by rain,
riding under the damp hills, carrying the color of the dawn.

Buster Keaton & the Cops

Stone Face is the likeness of all lovers.
Under a flower cart he keeps his seat
hiding his hopes from the crowd
until some clown discovers
his hat in the cop-cluttered street.

The officers fall on their knees. There
amid the flowers they find his hiding-place!
He remains undismayed...
He rubs his cuffs and dusts his collar.
The cops crawl up—they greet him face to face!

He throws roses in their eyes!
In retreat he duels for his life,
with daffodils he clouts their clubs.
Creeping from his cart, he tries
to lose them in the lilies which he spills.

Impeccably he plucks his hat
then races through the swirling street
while his shirt-tail flaps, unfurled,
and waves goodbye to his heart
and goodbye to the fragrant world.

The Red Bluff Rodeo

1
They travel the ranch roads that connect
with paved roads feeding into the freeway
to enter town by car or truck
or on horseback,
the main street blocked by traffic—
Not one empty seat in a bar and grill
for a mile around the fairgrounds.

"Let me have coffee and three eggs."
"How do you *like* your eggs?"
"I like 'em fine!"

2
       Clowns in costume (cow-
       boys, ranch hands)
       fall off
       a plow horse
       too old to mind the jeers
       of spectators. One clown
       climbs a cow, flings
       his feet in the air,
       slaps her rear and lifts
       his eyes to the sky,
       asking why she won't buck—
       Little laughter now
       people slide close,
       settling onto the wooden slats.

3
They roar for the first rider—
What's caught the eye of the crowd
is the swift stride of his horse
and the queer stiff legs of the calf.

His lasso loops her neck
to stop her short.
He drops beside her in the dust,
ties her legs tight with one length
of rope, and one twisted sweep of his arm.
Throws his hands in the air to show he's done,
like a man surrounded, forced to surrender.

Applause rattles the grandstand from its full height;
man and horse trot toward the gate.

The clowns come for the calf; hurry off.

The p.a. announces another number. The chute opens.
Out flies a fresh horse, a hat, hands
too quick for the calf
rolling helpless
in the grip of the rope.

4
Girls squirm in the sun.
Small boys turn their eyes
to women unwrapping
sandwiches. Wives
worried if a man might earn his entry fee
lean heads together
ignoring the noise, the nervous heat.

> "Did he come home sober last night?"
> "In the dark he tripped over a chair."
> "What did you do?"
> "I laughed so hard I fell out of bed."

5
The last man on a saddle bronc
provokes a rough ride

to impress the judges.
Jabbing flesh,
his spurs urge
the bronc to kick
three ways at once—

He flies from his mount
in mid-air, tossed
free. Falls
like a sack of meal in the dust.
The throng disapproves and boos.
On hands and knees he crawls away from the hooves.

    "Some sort of fun."
    "I'm glad it's done. All day
    I been dizzy as a squirrel."

The crowd staggers out of the stands,
pressing into the parking lot.

Evening dresses the country in cool stars.
Far in the night a fitful line of light
searches the length of the valley
where families follow one another home
beyond the lost barns and deserted fields.

Charlie Chaplin Has the Last Laugh

The scene suggests a city full of schemes.
The Tramp taps his cane *tip-pat, tip-pat,*
lolls by a lamppost looking at his shoes.
His pants are a bag of dreams.

His landlord, fat chin flapping on his collar,
struts down the street like a side of beef.
He wears a bulge of banknotes on his hip
and a smile like the crease in a fresh dollar—

A smile that drips with malice when he trips over
someone's cane
and gathers himself in a gutter
where the rainwater runs in a river.

The Tramp stares at his feet, feeling shy
at such success.
Left with his thumbing luck,
he buttons his ravelled vest to his fly.

He limps by like a man bent with bundles.
His black breast curves like a crow's.
But his wax-white eyes
flicker, flicker, as innocent as candles.

After His Assassination a Place of Peace

1
After his assassination a place of peace,
a church
impatient with piety,
pleas for Kennedy—
"Receive, receive, your servant Jack."
Lines of mourners murmur and turn back.
St. John's belfry wheel winds, and unreels its chimes.

The amber lamps upon the roof
of the radio tower pulse on and off.
Wire reports throughout the hour
grow like fine steel vines.

Through this electric speech a siren climbs
above the trees and screams
for the body borne away, given to the grass.

> Poor death, beggaring death,
> seeking a gift of us
> that has our breath.

In our restless peace
what can my hand touch
that will bloom?
Or our arms reach
that will bear?

2
Wind warps the shingled roofs slanting by the green
City Plaza where boughs storm;
winter oranges blaze like Christmas balls.

The green sign
of Christ will twine,
Love's wreath
cut from the tree of our wrath.

Everywhere we watch for this certainty.

The rain wells in the crotch of a walnut tree.

3
Water slides off a purple rib of the foothills,
lifting silt; it washes west,
it washes west through the tule marshes
and the brush-matted floor of the valley
and into the milling Sacramento River quietly spills.

4
Grief goes open in the street...
If we kill,
Sweet Christ,
who are free,
where is our peace?

What burns my blood away
in my own flesh?

Doves cower asleep
dry in the crowns
of green palms.

On the black airfield a radar cup waits.
Lights wink with power, clicking rise
along a low cloudbank, begin
their sweeping spin,
and death's found

day and night in each town
under drifting skies.

The valley rain chills my skin
and distracts and turns my dead legs,
and my spirit dead, growing into the winter of the war.

November carries cold across the land.
An inconstant sun. The sand coasts gripped in ice.

5
Dawn rises in the streets of our unrest.

While a pianist plays in his apartment
in the plaza we pause to listen,

strangers in a crowd caught by the cold strain
of music this morning,
as if memory might admire a deliberate refrain.

6
A raw rain, pouring, stains the skinned sycamores.
The rain crawls in the street, it looks insane,
it sits there, at noon, licked by dogs.

In the valley a late yield is marginal.
Water grass eats the profits out of the rice field.

All of this is so, but however it's seen, we know
there is a deep disorder now
between the eye and brain—

the cold spillage in the ditch between
what we can see
and what we can reach, and touch:

the ordinary darkness which accompanied the human
figures of men or women,
the company of others coming out on the river ground,

walking on a drying slope, overlooking the high water,
blades of wood awash in the mud-silt seeping
under a boat landing, and swelling into the delta.

7
Wet air gleams. After the rain the sunlight
is planked by a blue shade
that moves. A human
figure, man or woman,
a shadow-shape the sun casts in the grass.

My spirit's sorrow returns to town,
unable to follow its friend further,
as the shadow of our flesh falls before us.

Jets cross the missile silos
and a low bluff on the unchanneled salmon water
and ride tandem, then divide,
while the wind that was booming in the boughs
buries its breath in a pool.

8
After the rain leaves spawn and litter and stream.
Now they cling to the road in a flash chill like the first frost
on a ranch banked in blossoms.
Late warnings are broadcast;
the alert lamps smoke in the orchards.

When death drives us out of the solitary city
or town or prairie
we bring in our blood

the burden of the joy and anguish we see—

The spirit remembers the speed of a child,
grace in the veins,
the birds' timing—

A schoolboy fields a punt,
slips a tackler,
and he's free.

In the ranch air
and the deep farmland
the doves complain and hunt.

Small Moon on the Shoulder of New York

Small moon on the shoulder of New York—
In an alley children swim
against the dark. Some drift home.

Others remain among the stairs
and green garage doors

not one window lighted by a bulb
while they prolong their game,
choosing to search or sit hidden

in the narrow night. An hour later
the full moon on the rise

will find them here with its white eyes.
It finds my hands! My hair!
Hangs in my heart like a large lamp

leaving no shadow to hide your eyes
or the orb of each breast—

You occupy my mind like the moon!
The same light lands everywhere
outside the alley. The street corner

where a couple kiss before they cross
to the park. Pale moonlight

on the trees like water turns the leaves
to snow. This glow chills
my skin when I lie down alone—

The grass! The grass! Why is it so cold?
The long white grass of the moon—

The Sheep

1
On a green morning in spring we step out
a few feet at a time, stooping to eat
the top of the growing hill.
Beyond the end of each town
like the poor we are here at the edge
of everyone's sight, where we bow our heads
to the ground, going on with our meal.

2
We stand in the sun and eat through the summer.
Our coats are color of untreated clay.
We are the sheep the children see night and day.
They want to feel our fleece,
they want to hear what happens to all our wool.
Does it hurt to clip it? How fast will it grow? How does it
smell?

3
Each morning in fall we eat the cool hill
before the highway traffic appears.
Pairs of headlights reach into the rain.
Tall trucks follow the cars which whine
past the posted signs—
                              For years
the land has been for sale
but no buyers. The soil
too dry in summer
and wet all winter.

4
Let winter arrive we are ready
to outwait every trouble man knows—
snow in the foothills, a flood in the valley,

or the freezing spell that turns his wells to ice—
with no thought for his grief, happy in this life,
alone with our own hunger and as lasting as the grass.

The Land of the Dead

A shimmer of summer
heat haunts the county road before dark.
Cars rattle flat out until they skid
down a dusty grade
to stop by the pines.
Doors clap open—
Four men climb out
slipping away from the warm fear of America.

Scrub pine fills a forest as green as rain.
On the riverbed
of red clay the grass has gone to seed.

From here men have escaped
to the other world,
the land of the dead.
Their bodies disappear
down a grassy rise,
the eyes of their souls
look back and see the moon
like a barge, built with bones, floating on the field.

More black men sit whispering
on the fishing pier
with their lines strung in the river,
boat and oars
half-hid downshore
and the moon rowing over the grass forever.

You Are Never Happy

America, you are never happy, and slowly
the season freezes like a lake in heaven.
Leaves unfold flying in a blizzard blowing
wings of yellow wax to garment the grass.

There are shapeless weights in the weather all winter.
You are never happy, yesterday you thought
about the thickness of things that have no bark
or handles no you are never happy.

You are worried when the sunlight leans uneasy
and understanding the State Department
is like moving mattresses, you are never happy,
there are shapeless weights in the weather all winter.

The cherry trees refuse to freeze at the close
of Congress, they remember Lincoln angry
at last, lunging at Seward; saying,
"Any man over forty is responsible for his face!"

Slowly the time forms like ice in heaven
where saints skate shaving off the domes of the clouds,
sending us snow spraying down all day
on white wings of wax though you are never happy.

Geese Going North

They fight to be free of our earth,
legs dangling, drawn up in the driving air,
wings stroking the wind, beating its current beneath the keel
of the breastbone as they're borne
toward that loud height
where we find them this morning in full flight.

On an April morning they ride
our warm wind from the south,
so many that all I can hear is their cry—
Canada Geese and Blues and Snows,
thousands squawking in the sky
while they flash over fields that weathered the winter.

On into noon they pass
in formation along the flyway.
They flock down to feed,
attracted by acres of corn or barley,
eager to graze on fresh grain or grass.
Once more they climb the wind—

They soar like a man who has flown
free of his thought,
happy to shed his shadow,
his dark image drifting alone
on swift wings over the earth. Wings which carry
the clamorous speed of the birds

farther than eyes can listen
for their long calls flying
out of the day and the fecund land
where our flesh follows.
As though to enclose the cool lake
below their voices

a pine forest grows
more green and remote when it rises.
Geese glide through these trees to reach the shore.
At rest on the water, wide wings withdrawn,
they float over the lake in its last light,
blue pool of the soul that deepens with the night.

What Is the Wild Love That Leads Us?

What is the wild love that leads us down
to the end of the flat canyon floor,
cluttered with leaves and branches blown
to earth and rotting in the rain,

urging us onto this trail,
tracking for mile after mile?
The rain holds behind us until
we stumble to find our footing where

we've waded into the iron cold snow
that all but covers a mountain meadow.
What is the wild love that leads us far
away from the long land below,

the hunt forgotten in the autumn air
full of flakes? By dark the storm
has died down and we see moonlight bloom
across the ridge. When we climb

beyond the prints of the small brown bear
and the last clean tracks of the deer
and fall into a circle by the fire,
what is the wild love that leads us here?

SCENES FROM CHILDHOOD

And we are put on earth a little space
That we may learn to bear the beams of love.

—William Blake

The Thief's Niece

While the women sliced brown bread and cold meat
the thief's niece unrolled a winding sheet.
Old men leaned at the wall to count
how many masked guards the growers
hired for the ride. She walked out so hers
was the first face he might see from his mount
now it came groping into the black street.

Between two guards the council-treasurer
whispered to the priest to comfort her.
She heard the horses climbing through the dark.
The girl said there were no growers to be found—
"They have their money back." On high ground
one guard reined in his horse to mark
a limb's width. The old men haunched where they were.

The guard riding out front held the pistol
her uncle had fired—shot up the hotel
lobby, wounding a clerk. He roped the limb—
"Pray!" the girl begged. "Pray he may live!"
The priest explained, "Mercy is relative…
Yes, we'll pray now." The coroner behind him
bowed his head. Then the elders from the council.

The wives and girl sat by the tree. Nearby
the guards and jailor on horse watched the sky.
At dawn the first guard cut the councilman's
horse with a belt. It bolted and he hung
while they rode downhill. Then his friends among
the growers' younger sons and the farmhands
drew down upon his heels to help him die.

The Brooding Child

In my dream the brooding child
I was ten years ago leans far
back, tilting his kitchen chair,
to hear the Chicago Symphony
of the Air. No one else is home
until the strings and horns fall still.
A sudden crowd swarms the room—
Grey-eyed uncles and aunts, and Father
and Mother. My sister Julia, too.
It might be every holiday reunion.
If I were younger I would guess
my First Communion. It's not,
though someone has invited Father Tein,
who thought he was a friend of mine.

Their faces are flames that glow
without the weight of guilt.
Their voices know my name—
"Gerhardt!" they cry. Or simply
"Gary!" if it's my sister. Always
I look as if I'm listening.
Now they command my attention
their mouths form an important shape—

    "You can be anyone you want.
    Anyone at all!"

                I smile.
They blaze into ordinary air.
Why should they stay? I recall
their message vividly. They dare
not fester in restless sleep
like some hallucination out of Hell.
Mostly they're my family, you see.

And because I was taught every dream
is a delusion, telling you this
just now I smiled. Still
in the dream I understand they mean
what they say: "Be anyone at all"

but not that child.

The Tempest Sonata

A grey day in April—
Thunder fills the wells to the brim.
Tall elms tremble.
We walk the orchard road to the grave of my uncle.

Our parents hurry us home, the storm
swells in the wind—
Over the turned earth
it sets the fields on fire,
flashing bright and black.

>Let my body break
>its solitude
>and speak in
>song, in spirit
>with the throbbing air.

I trudge into my mother's study.
The piano is enormous furniture.
The art of playing is to make it disappear—

Why do we say
we play music? It isn't play,
this melody I make for my sister—

I want her music to fly free of my body
unable to bear the stern stillness
before the first note
like the low sky before rain—

I want her not to see
the boy beating on the keys, weeping
with wild, delicious dread—

Afraid of the beauty within
men and women, how could I know
we are ourselves piano, woodwind, horn?

Too late we learn the throat is the magic flute—
With every breath our dying words are sung.

This Field, This Lake

Over Rock Lake this morning, all morning
the sun levitates like a lucky kite.
At noon we untie it from the pier.
Birds row their voices across the day.

How can the place of our birth be wrong?
Born in blood, we know the near
tide pulse, or pull. Its surge and sway
until the rag-tailed sun takes flight.

Though all birds follow and disappear
behind the sky, our souls at play
plead: O let us live day and night
blazing in the body where we belong—

This field of flesh, this lake of light
about us is our being, but we hear
dark music in the mind and steal away
deep into night where we sing, we sing.

THE BURNING BEAR

*Touching the human body is
almost like touching heaven.*

—Novalis

In the Sky Are Two Bears

Stars
that trail their blood
over the ice of our eyes.

Their shaggy legs weightless
at winter's end
stumbling

out of the steaming caves of space.

That pair who live by the pattern of their luck
which makes them walk a little drunk
on the wine of dusk

never one without the other
always pursuing.
Always apart.

Did I Tell You?

Did I tell you the heavens are watching, waiting?
When we wandered out of the woods
the road home led far
away from where we kissed.
Where we found our first bed.
But never is the night a danger. Never
is the day. This is what we see
of heaven. Now the sun. Now these stars
alive with light, like what awaits us.
                         Did I tell you
the heavens are watching? In broad day
you climbed the blue roof to paint your eyes
everywhere, yes, the sun slid down and I saw them
over me... Now it is so bright
so many stars flame above us
a few are falling. Rocketing down the dark
they pierce the universe and disappear...
                         Still many remain.
There shines your Bear. There stalks mine.
                         Did I tell you
every point of the Bear's body is on fire?
And his black flesh, like life, is larger than life.
Listen, did I tell you
the world is spinning in its green space
to hold us together, although it is winter, dim and wet.
And the heavens are watching, weeping. Did I tell you that?

The Burning Bear

How long will the fire leap? How high?
Why ask the wood? You're the woman
who touched its tinder, saw smoke climb.
Flames flung their arms around our bones.

Tonight no moon—
How the Bear glitters!
Each bone a torch
blazing on the border of his life.

Nowhere can this captive Bear escape
his perimeter of pain.
Fire is all we see
of him. Fire is all

the form he feels, his broad limbs glow.
His hide black from haunch to head,
he prowls the snow of stars
until he knows his mate is near—

Flame of her flesh, light of her voice
in the charred sky! His claws curl,
his eyes crack like coal—
He burns, he burns. He will never die.

Your Eyes

1
Lightning crackles over us. That first flash
backlights the woods and turns black
red maples, golden aspen.
In your eyes their dusty leaves are doused with rain.
Eyes of earth and night,
a cat's eyes
in the dark glowing
with silence like these pools
the storm fills in the open woods.

2
How lucky you are you can't see your eyes.
Only their image a glass pond returns—

I see them
when I swim
to the surface for air.

3
In the heart of the storm we hold each other.
Your hands are cool like the rain.

Look how the wind drives the rain
beyond the canyon. . . Slowly
through the dripping trees
the thick brown bear without its mate,
burrs caught in its coat,
lumbers down the mudpath to the river.

4
Woman of flickering lamps, paths, and the night sky.
I take your hand and we cross the clearing—
We kiss in the wet grass,

your eyes downcast.
Fearful, quick, like the deer you prefer
shadows
not this sudden slant of light.
The gravel road into town glints in the late sun.

5
Twilight falls among the turning leaves,
the ruin of trees, red and gold.
A blood-red wind blows through the streets—
A wild wind! The whole town trembles.
What are you looking at?
Streetlights flare on one by one.

Those tossing trees. Maples. Elms.
Behind your eyes a flame breathes
into the solitary house its gleam—
And this smoke in my throat when you speak.
We put out the lamp
by the bed and the autumn night turns
black, in our souls
red leaves leap in the wind.

Love, Listen . . .

In the cold quiet of the stars
what whispers
is the night asleep
beneath my tongue and yours.

Joy

The storm blunders through the street, flapping
every awning. A downpour drenches
shoppers caught on the walks, the clerk
on her hurried errand, whipping her skirt
against her legs. Together we reach
the aged bandstand, shingles gone
from a gaping roof, the only shelter
in the green plaza. One summer night
Sidney Bechet played here,
his clarinet singing that sad joy
that was his voice. Is it the wind
or rain that makes you laugh? We lean
close. Your hand in my coat. What
a storm! Black elms blaze! The wind roars
on, roars on, tossing branches. Rain
batters the empty benches.
                                        Step back,
look. Water from the splayed roof spills
splat splat around our feet.
Yes, and your hair! How it shines!
How happy I am you're here! But this rain!
It's so loud we turn to watch the wind
buffet the roses, the hyacinths. Now
it plunges down the footpath, shaking
all the shrubbery, bright as silver.
It takes hold of the blue phonebooth
by the flowerbed—a wobbly glass
door swings open, claps shut. Rain swamps
the blossoms. We love each other, we can't
speak. I hold you and we shiver like the grass.

Thunder Storm

Wind rocks our tent. The storm
staggers among the trees.
High in the cave of night
the two Bears roll over, thunder
rumbles down. Why
did we quarrel? We curl up,
my knees in the hollows of yours,
my hand on your mound. Love,
I kiss your neck and you laugh.
Against my thighs I feel
your flesh push and give.
Late at night we listen
to the rain, falling asleep.

Our tent, drenched, gleaming,
leans in that green hush
before morning. How long
since we heard the rain
stop? Quiet, still drowsy,
we stroke each other. *Whik-
whik, whik-whik.* What's that?
We sit up, unzip the flap—
In the dripping light the trees
breathe birds into the sky.

Black Water

Black blazing night. My heart
pounding, I hear
your heartbeat under my hand,
we pause beneath the trees
to kiss. Hike on down
from the high woods.
Loud
rush of wings. Wind falling
silent in the pines. You and I
follow the old bear trail trampled
clear to the shore: Rocks,
rubble, sedge grass tall
in the shallows. No moon
on the lake. Stars
spark and shine.
Alone
through the dark we watch
two ducks tuck in, drift together.
On the pine shore we lie down—
I want to feel your breasts turn
firm in my palm. Your tongue
in my mouth when our legs open.
In the moist fur the fold
encloses me. And when we part
I want to lie with you
the way night lies on deep water—
On the slow breathing lake
two wild ducks float
side by side, asleep
on still water. Black water.

EARTH'S EYE

A lake is the landscape's most beautiful and expressive feature. It is earth's eye, looking into which the beholder measures the depth of his own nature. . . .

—Henry Thoreau, *Walden*

Rain

August watches from the porch, one hand
spread upon the screen like a star.
No stars. Lightning flares. He hears
both his hounds prowling around the pond.
Thunder disturbs the brim
where his wife's chrysanthemums
color the water with their blooms:
Red rust, egg yolk, white plaster.

Every blossom is a gaudy crown
unwilling to bow
to the ground
in the gravity of rain.

The odor of a dark storm
swarms
in her hair, unribboned,
tumbling down her lilac gown.
In bed they listen to the rain
rattle the whole house now.
Roof, walls, porch, pasture.
All the earth saturated, shaken, still—

How long her hair is
rolling over his shoulder.
This is what he will remember after
forgetting her flowers. (There in the rain

they bow.)

A World Apart

Julia's brother wrote
his final song for her
before his plane was lost
over Africa, in the war.

Time and again she sang—
Her friends, her family
listened long in the shade.
Starlings flocked to the tree.

She taught us Africa meant
mad elephants, dry air
on fire. The grasses lean
and brown, the mudholes bare.

Birds of brilliant plumage
shrieking: *Planes that roar
out of the dawn to strafe
the tents on the burning floor.*

*They shell the tanks. Oil drums
ignite. Two planes attack
the water trucks and vanish
in a black burst of flak—*

Skoronsky the young scholar
argued, "No analogy
ever should be drawn
from war's brutality."

But Julia disagreed:
"In this world every soul
knows the pain of birth—
The great beast or the small

child or whistling bird
Each life is strange and frail
and suffers its sudden death,
human and animal."

"Clearly," Skoronsky scoffed,
"a culture ruled like ours
by rational thought and will
is a world apart from theirs."

And he left her by the starlings
that trilled their reckless tune
while elephants came walking
through the brittle afternoon.

If April

If April is to green the earth again
Rock Lake will unlock with shuddering sighs
when love lies down with death in the dark rain

easing the ice, so the slow floes drain
into the swelling stream. We'll hear it rise,
if April is to green the earth again

where the willows stir, shaking that satin sheen
from their stiff skirts, the fine snow from our eyes.
Though love lies deep with death in the dark rain

rumpling their bed, on the blue mud we've seen
the first loon wade, or waddle, before he flies.
If April is to green the earth again

soon will that demon deep-diving loon
shatter the water with his witless cries.
Must love lie still as doom in this dark rain?

The lake's awake! We hear the hooting loon,
loud, loud, beneath our somber skies—
If April is to green the earth again,
Love, we'll lie warm and laugh in the dark rain.

In Early Spring

1

In early spring I felt the weight
of his legs
upon my own. I undid my dress,
we watched the wind row
across the water. At once then all
my dread
began. As if my soul
grew wary, troubled by the low splash
of the lake, and the chill that gripped the earth

where we lay beneath a curtain
of willows.
I leaped up to leave. Brushing, then, my
clinging clothes, afraid
he would force me down. Still I delayed,
I stroked
the cold light on his hair,
looking into the leaves, asking now
how will I live? What will become of me?

2

No, she told me! *No, we'll be lost*!
Fanned the fresh
wrinkles from her damp dress, fled uphill
and drove home. Her car
buzzing behind the webs of trees and blazing
water. Waiting, I saw
a second couple nimbly climbing
down the steep hill and straying toward the shore.

I tried tracing the chains of young
leaves, restless,
eager for her. The ache like a rock

sinking in my sex.
If the face of God is ecstasy
it is
a membrane of moist light
throbbing in the willows, and I won't
save myself, I have always lived like this.

The Quarrel

1
Our basket is shut, wax wrappings packed in it.
    Coffee and the gold cans of ale
        drunk, while we quarrel alone.

Only a mile east of the village limit
    pickups, vans, cars, transport the pale
        light into late afternoon.

We rise. Your coat. The basket. Wait one minute
    while a brisk wind troubles the trail
        those two horses amble down.

2
Green the shade, green and yellow the blowing grass
    their pasture yields, where the quick course
        of Rock Creek has carved its width

side to side, through bottomland gentle as moss.
    How we'd like to drop our remorse
        in the cool grass. Down the path

the mare loiters shy. The stallion loping past
    crops her mane, and the courted horse
        happily tramples the earth.

Spring Is the Smallest Thing We Know

Spring is the smallest thing we know, the least
noise we listen to is the speech of bees,
who cruise a field for clover and as they pass
whisper *science* to the tacit grass—

grass that multiplies around a man
remembering damp shadows on the land
this spring and every spring until he dies;
grass that grows like rain before our eyes.

Rain is the longest law we've ever seen;
taller than all our thoughts of trees, the rain
reduces every distance, dear, to here,
where we lie waiting for the wind to clear

a sullen sky and bring the singing wren—
this bird who stirs such music in the sun
he wakes our dim world from its winter trance,
and makes your warm legs dream and my hands dance.

Love May Be Glad

The clear eye of the lake—
Once it was the only witness
to dragonflies flitting over the water.
Her hand on his, her touch as light as theirs.

Who heard their whispers that summer evening?
The wind was up.
On a taut rope their boat nodded *yes*,
slipped its mooring and drifted into dusk.

Pretty pictures please us, until we see
where the stern struck rock.
Thrust up on shore
in winter the prow pockets snow,
The eye all ice now.

Ice too has its say. It says stay
close to the cold fact
that shelters fantasy and keeps it deep
until the lake unlocks
this story in time.

A story telling us

the eye is ours
open to the blue or blank
with cold. Telling us

love may be glad and green
in a world as brief as this,
as brutal as their words were beautiful.

The Boat

1
Where is the woman who unmoored this morning,
rowing upriver to visit her sister?
Toward noon her skiff rides so high
its keel climbs free of the current.

No one to work the oars,
they drag silver ribbons like whispers
her children trail through the sedge grass.

2
Into blue shadow her boat
drifts under the arch of the stone bridge.

3
The boat brightens floating in crimson light,
more earth than air in it.

Light at the last hour
downstream where the yolk of the sun breaks,
bleeding in the water.

The River's Sister

Emil Mueller, M.D.:

Hunters' trucks, my black wagon, the sheriff's car,
idle now. We gather by the river,
we hear its hum and wonder
what was the pain you couldn't bear?
Reporters approach with cameras and tape—
Our somber column crawls through the fields into town.

An aging man with a wife and unwed daughter,
I have questions beyond procedure
a coroner's practice fails to answer.
The autopsy is obscure: No scars.
No bruises, contusions.
Belly not bloated. Neither
pregnant again nor long in the water.

How easily loneliness enters the soul,
as lightly as a young mother steps
into a little boat. It faintly sways
to the pull of oars as she disappears
beneath the brown willows only
to float into my helpless hands—

Sister of the river,
you are sorrow endless and young, silence
with no one to forgive.
You are what cannot be saved by our learning or love.
At the end of your journey I wait
to greet you with my dumb grief—
You are with us always but you never arrive.

In The Sanitarium of the Sacred Heart

"I saw spirits gliding among the flames"
Purgatorio XXV

White flurries immerse
the day. March weather
darkens, dusk combs her cold hair.
Lord, how have I sinned
if Little Boy brought this peace?
Sister says, *Lie down.*

Wake to hear the robin sing
in the maple: *Spring! It's Spring!*

The breezy day-nurse
skips by, her sweater
swirling over her shoulder—
April night. That wind,
pursuing dark flocks of geese,
at dawn drops the moon.

Squirrels so red they scorch the trees
interrupt these reveries—

While a blue jay screams
in an oak the priest
brings bread. Down the winding drive
the gardener's fire
crackles and alarms the loud
bird fleeing the oak,

piercing the shade with his fear
of the flapping flames. I hear

his cry in my dreams.

These visions, Sister,
persist: 8/6/45
        as we climb higher
into heaven, the black cloud
        boiling. Cinders, smoke.

Hiroshima burns beneath
the blind wind, city of death

        in life, the slim child
        bleeding from her ears.
The blank face of her mother
        broiled pink, no mouth left
to cry. They hear such shrill pleas
        all doctors ignore

these silent cases: A man's eyes
melt in their sockets; horseflies

        attack his flesh. Mild-
        mannered, he appears
with those long dead who gather
        in my sleep. I wet
my sheets and fall to my knees,
        sobbing on the floor.

Maples harden. Cold nights drift
into Advent. Now the gift

        of a damp snow drapes
        the motor-test wing
and clinic garden. I've seen
        from my window-loft
every blade of ice a knife
        honed to carve my soul

from this flesh! And Nature still
dares to teach us how to heal—

       At noon in blue capes,
         white gloves, boots, three young
nurses slant across the lawn.
         The tall girl looks lost
in thought. Then I hear her laugh,
         lighter than the snow.

In the Eternal Present All Things Are

floating on
the Rock River, green limbs and rippling
images of limbs
dragging leaves in the quarrelsome current.
You listen to
their hissing, you
hear it as discontent,
mindful of midsummer
air, muggy, sullen; a slowly shifting sky
where you see a hawk hover, far and deep.

The hawk rows
in a warm wind across the orchard
acre crows nest in
to the elm and oak woods behind the lake.
While the rain swells
around her, she hunches low in an oak
dry under the near limbs:
she is the jump into the wind, the brown glide
and the fall to green cover, braked and steep.

The full length
of the riverbed the rain searches
the murky water:
no rowboats, outboard motors. Just upstream
turbines turn eight
generators
3,600
rpm, spinning off
a small waterfall, the spillage coursing out
to the stone-blue lake in a silent sweep.

When the trout
sinks in dark water two fishermen

laugh, turning. They hoist
their poles up the steps of the power plant,
watching a hawk
fly the green woods
to the river. The rain
blows by. Beside a rock
the trout rides, holding under the current his
sudden lunge, the rise, the swift silver leap.

Waiting for Winter

1
I think of my name, Julia Grahm,
and hold my hands so in a circle,
making my mind obey my mind.
Alone in a harsh room in some home,
no sound but my breathing for hours.
Light cleanses the floor of its color.
On the walls no mirrors, no chairs
in the corners or tables or flowers.

My flesh has forsaken its shadow.
My eyes wander to one window
which offers a view of the orchard,
apples and pears long since picked
and packed. Leaves purple the grass.
Rubbed to its sheen like a pewter plate,
behind bare branches sleeps the lake.

In all that ache of autumn
the only woman—Why must I wait
for the weather to turn? And turn again?
Caught up in a crowd of acquaintances
I want to feel the wishes of my flesh
though I know that I'm dreaming—
No one is here, no one is coming.

2
It's impossible to move one muscle
even to music, unless you love.
Look at me, I want to see
the swift sex of birds!
Spring sun melting the mud!
To be born in a warm season like the bulbs—
The first sound of sin that you hear in your skin.

However, it's almost the end
of November and over blue fields
flakes are sown or scattered without care.
A pocket of snow collects in the crotch
of every available tree,
and I'm frozen in my fortieth year
of this dream, waiting for winter.

I keep my wits. I say I'm a wise woman.
Then an ice storm strikes so deep
it chokes the spring in the lake for weeks
and won't warm. Well water sleeps.
The orchard claws at the wind.
My bones are blind but they believe
what they are told of cold despair.
Now it is coming, now it is here.

At Julia's House

Carollers leave the drifting road. To reach
Julia's house they weave like mourners in a row

crossing the burial ground beyond her barn.
For miles around the rising tide of snow

floods the farms. . . When the boys halt, the girls
lean in their woolen arms. Their candles quake and glow.

They wait, whispering steam. Like lantern lights
they shadow and gleam until they sway

her mind. Still she perches in the rose
window-seat to learn if they will stay.

Now her only choice is to listen for their singing,
she cannot hear their voices, and why do they delay?

To Bring Spring

Free of their scarves, their woolen coats,
   girls toss their hair
     in the gun-blue dusk,
      dancing on
the porch. Laughter spills
   over the lawn; a breeze tails
    off Rock Lake cold
     with the steel smell
of rainwater. Frail
   lanterns in the paper evening air
    blow half-way dark
     and half-way back.

Late in the morning a dead season lies
   hardly glimmering
    on the hill. Or
      leans at the porch in the sun.
Robins bob beside the mud; green
   shoots sprout in the pasture.
    The white colt, his winter legs
     slack, strolls
up from his hay, deliberately
   he trudges the sodden hill. Down
    and up the rise
     apple branches blossom.

A slow girl, her black hair braided,
   and two tall sisters strip
    the lanterns off. The sisters
     with a certain arch,
like divers, loft
   the lamp shells down
    to their friend. All three walk out
     the drive as sunlight blows

under the eaves. The last girl
    cradling several globes
        in her bare arms,
            yellow and blue and rose.

These Small Songs

Suppose we are unaware of time passing.
And all our hours are expended passing
into time. Soon, it's summer. This
green evening strung with cicada song.
A boat droning across our violet sleep.

Let it seem to. We'll wake and walk
into a warmer morning. We are
passing into time. If only
on the stony shore where we are.

Where pines hold one pose
hour by hour
against an unblinking glare,

their rare restraint
visible since noon
in that reflective light in which they lean

toward dusk
when a blue sun floats over
Rock Lake and
noiseless they

dive.
    Splash-

less shadows lengthen,
swimming far from shore.
Swimming their darkness over the water
not like a leaky net drawn
by a droning boat. More like night
itself, which catches and holds

the soul's attention. Utterly still

but for the boat. And these small songs
the cicadas sing, constant as clocks
that tell of something passing. Let it.

THE STARRY MESSENGER

Love is the highest religion.

—Ibn ʿArabi

The Astronomer's Childhood
and Early Youth

1
His father Vincenzo—a musician—had fallen out of favor
with the only nobles who might hire him—ever.
Hot-tempered, quick to curse, he drank each cup
of his disgrace among his family. Daily
a red-faced rage frightened his wife and son.

About the boy: Born in Tuscany
and christened Galileo Galilei
when he grew into his thick body
and blunt speech
his hair, like his father's, had a fiery luster.

Never a scholar
though inquisitive from his first breath
(his mother vowed)
in time he became a loud quarrelsome youth
contrary, she thought, to his tender nature.

Children of shrewd merchants and comfortable landowners
called him—to his face—a conceited ass
though his parents were ashamed of their poverty.

2
In the neighborhood. In the shadows of the abbey.
"Bastard!"
Boys spit on his knobby hands.
"Dunce!"
Until he adapted a metronome to time the human pulse.

A ready brawler,
he fought them

often
weeping
before he was struck

for he lived in fear
of the vicious kick
or sharp rock.

He too hit hard
and if his strength failed him he flailed on
but blinded by tears
he was beaten to his knees
in the street. In the schoolyard.

3
When he sold his design for a military compass
he presented the money to his mother.

4
Because his genius was for dynamics
he invented a hydrostatic balance—

5
Finding the frequency of its return depends upon the length
of the object departing
("Does this apply . . .?")
he devised the first pendulum for a clock.

6
However tutors found him unteachable:
"He thinks with his fists!"
He was denied a scholarship to Pisa.

"Others may kiss a man's cloak.
I labor like an ox—
No rest from the yoke."

7
Nobles, a few, took notice. Churchmen, too.

Night and day he educated his eye
to discern the exact progress
of objects in motion,
whether linear or orbital.

Bristling at each rebuke,
he advanced swiftly
with a passionate will
because he improved on the efforts of modest mechanics.

"A prepared mind works the most potent magic
this side of our dreams. And death."
So thought an enlightened Cardinal del Monte.
And, yes, it was he
who commended the anxious youth to the Duke of Tuscany:

"Yet, one wonders, can he learn accommodation?
Or is he, alas, more trouble than he's worth?"

The Whispering City

1
Galileo is astonished that a full-grown man might find
    himself
staring childlike at the evidence—simple, irrefutable—
which each day offers. As when he observes
the force which pumps blood through his veins
lifts the dawn
dripping from the canals of Venice,
surprising the doves with a sudden shower.

The sky clears—and what can he learn of the doves?
The flock aloft now in the light.
How they welcome the air, trust it, abandon themselves to
it.

How they soar unburdened beneath the morning sun.

2
    Nature asks us
    what is matter?
    Does energy travel
    a continuous curve?

    What creature, therefore,
    truly knows peace?
    Is ever at rest?

    He watches fishermen
    haul their catch
    onto the dock—a web

    of troubled abundance,
    writhing, silver
    sides swollen until

the purling net
sags, pulls apart,
pours its dazzle
flapping into the cart.

3
A man of no little faith,
he believes life is eternal
energy, boundless in body and soul,
as the sun ministers to the whispering city:

First it disperses shadows, then, dexterously
as a rose opens
it dries the stones
on the Piazza San Marco and they blaze like bronze!

Venice: the Morning Market Opens

It's daybreak and he's almost sober. Soon the pride
of the Cathedral—its carillon—will beckon
the faithful to matins. God, how he loves this hour!
Not the mist lifting in first light from the *laguna*
but the way the water wakes the lusty city
with a low voice—sultry and violent as hers—
while it wears the dawn like Dutch damask upon
the bodice of his mistress, no longer young, arranging
her hair; abundance rippling with each motion.
To hell with those who tell you the study of Nature
is not the study of Power! Galileo hears
the slow current shifting through the channel
of San Nicolo; in a moment the market—six hundred
tents and stalls—will open its arms
to the harbor. Heaven and earth offer all
the cargo a man desires. Weighted with grain,
Arabian horses, gunpowder, lumber—teak
and cedar—opium, salt, Siberian furs,
stowaways in the hold too frightened to speak,
ships rock at anchor on the glittering water.

Bronze bells clang, clang. He smiles. The market stirs.

Tintoretto

Because he believes
perspective is a useful illusion
deftly it lifts the veil

from the soul
and we see all that happens
in one world happens in the other—

Painting the *Crucifixion*,
Tintoretto urges us to trust our eyes
to guide us

under the storm-tossed trees
to the bald hilltop
and they spare us nothing:

Not the princes, priests, merchants;
even the powerful are curious—
at a distance they sit their mounts.

Not the whirl of spectators which includes
the complaisant dog
watching the man with the spade.

Not the two soldiers rolling dice,
six laborers binding a thief to a cross,
the circle of mourners collapsed beneath their grief.

Look—here is Jesus hanging by his hands.
Stakes are driven through his hands and feet.
A soldier prepares to stab him with a spear.

We see Jesus' head is bowed.
Too late at the foot of the cross

a woman strains to hear his last words.

From his throat a cry
has been torn—
it chills the air we breathe.

Look—
though the worst is done
there is no limit to our fears.

The vault of heaven itself lies broken.
Lightning is about to strike
from the yellow sky

which appears over Golgotha.
Its gleam yields
little warmth

on the wild hill
where men and women weeping
embrace each other

without shame.
This is how we join the just
and the unjust—

This is how we find our way
in the world men have made
as if we were gods.

Adriatic Evening

When dusk deepens   over the sea   and the sky
shimmers   the long-striding day   with its sacred
sense of possibility   departs.   As the last light
withdraws   into an Adriatic evening   the woman
      steps
deliberately over   drenched blue stones.   Spilling from
mollusk shells,   washing out of swollen   sea
      anemone,
a coarse sand,   bronze and black,   swirls at her feet.

The man beside her   sees   even the stragglers
among the gulls are rising   scrabbling   into the air
before he understands   it is absence   that sustains
their cries and loss   is not the end of love.
Walking down the shore   they trail the gulls
expecting night   to overtake them   but the birds
wander out to sea   where   in a single thought

they settle among the waves   rocking to sleep
as the hour continues   darkening   within
its burnished border   while it unfolds   a plush
beauty almost   beyond belief   like the robe
of a scandalous pontiff   seen for what it is
and still it is so   elaborately spread
before them   upon the water in purple splendor.

Stellar Dominions

*In a notebook seized prior to his execution by
agents of the Inquisition, Giordano Bruno
asserts a limitless universe and questions the
reliability of all optical perception...*

Because each of us is a creature of the unfathomable
God, we are formed, sweet friends, in the likeness
of that exquisitely inventive sovereign
Lord who (unutterably alone)
occupies one vast
Heaven among the hundred million heavens.

For just as you and I are a world within a world
so, too, many galaxies—stellar dominions—must grow
like fires that flare up in a black and endless forest

(for such is the forest of the night):

conflagrations which ignite and so acquire
(every one according to its nature)
a serviceable shape

only to die
a slowly blazing death
beyond our comprehension

but never beyond
the mind of the one
Creator who brought them forth.

O, my clever companions, tell me:
How is the immense mystery
of a truly solitary

God to be revealed
or refuted?

Honor our striving if not our success. . .

For within us arise walls more formidable than stone and
mortar.
Within the prison of each person exist many cells
inhabited by—would you say—angels or demons?
Are we not then the agents of our own doom or bliss?

What might I confess
that I dare not
act out
in the dusky light of every thought?

For in the mind of any man or woman dwells
not a trickster
but a diligent
reverent
and cunning magician.

For if the eye shares its curvature
with the everywhere bending earth
then indeed our slightest observation
(like the most intricate sighting)
requires infinite adjustment—

Imagine,
my brothers, my sisters,
how little we see clearly and without distortion.

In the Monastery Garden

Love is not longing it is action—
The six novices in the monastery garden know this

and it makes them furious.
They swear between their teeth.

On their knees
in soil wet with last night's rain

to weed the bean rows
with no breakfast this morning but bitter coffee.

In anger the six hiss like a swarm of black bees
while they pull the weeds.

Herons

Herons thrive in Ostia where no ship sails
into harbor. Fishnets fray. Unknot. Return
to stray hemp—threads for nests. Once a port fails

to satisfy the Roman soul merchants spurn
its market. More marsh than river, the Tiber sprawls
before us. Frogs roil the shallows. Here, we learn,

the Emperor Hadrian wept. Among wine halls
Augustine remembered his lost life. Here,
down a wharf thick with shops, makeshift stalls,

Pope Urban led his blind astrologer.
Rain threatens and a homing heron calls
its mate. Together they approach the shore

where a resplendent shrine, neglected, falls
to ruin: while the last mosaics break
the lusty gods cavort across these walls—

Noon finds them lying shattered in the wake
of a black squall. Already summer trails
Hadrian into history. Herons rake

the marsh. At dusk they roost among the scales
on the docks of Ostia, where no ship sails.

Carnevale

1
Into the torch-lit square
nine musicians stream
with spangled timbrels,
a lute, a violin,
the rising thrum
of a Spanish guitar,
three burnished horns
and an eel-skin drum.

Hundreds in costume dance
in their wake—the prison
cook flaunts the billowing
mauve sleeves of a countess.
Mad boars. Mermaids. Marching
bears. Barbers wearing rouge;
butchers, priests, street-
thieves. Merchants' wives
clutching house-pets.
Pimps, jugglers, acrobats.

A jet-haired gypsy
rider—she's thirteen
and out of sorts
with this jostling
throng—tucks her
head down, flings
both feet skyward,
naked belly taut
but slender legs
waggling slightly,
sustaining her
uncertain balance,
palms pressed upon

the tawny back of
her pony trotting
into a dim side-street.

2
The courtesan confined
by her ponderous black
robe—tonight she's Chief
Magistrate—frees one
arm from its velvet fold,
shaking her tambourine.

The bearded bride, so coy
beside her buxom groom—
a blacksmith and his wife.
His white gown almost splits;
she traipses in borrowed
boots and trousers. They kiss,
then share a belly-laugh.

Behind the blind mule
wearing a bishop's mitre
four whores stroll
happily
bare-breasted
scattering flowers.

Music first and last.
Riding in the green
and red three-wheel cart
drawn by his stepson
the man with no legs
strums a mandolin.

3
In the marketplace a proud Arabian
stallion glowers over
his timbered stall
at the modest mare
penned next door.

Milanese armor gleams
no less than saddlery tooled
in silver. Subtler flames
linger in a display of amber
brooches. At open tents
fish for sale. Fresh-
baked bread. Piping little
pigs battle each other
for scraps. Caged birds
entertain us with trills.
Wineskins and swollen
sausages sway overhead.

Tubs of olive oil.
Casks of honey.

An orange cat stretches, yawns, rubs
the lavender leg
of the Grand Duchess of Tuscany,
a prostitute in a disheveled dress

accompanied by the bald courtier
bearing a mirror (hers or his?)
in which he admires the fading image
of a middle-aged Narcissus.

4
The cat strolls away.
It's abruptly caught

up, nuzzled, and
hidden in his thin shirt
by a frightened boy who steals purses.

Their tunics trimmed
with ivy, two
slender youths
play wooden flutes.

5
Wine awakens the ardent fake
Franciscan abbot—by day
a devout bureaucrat—
to her animal nature:
this two-legged lioness
leaning into his hands
as they undo her dun-
colored costume down
to undulating hips.
Her tail's a lithe
length of rope which
twitches with glee.
"There's nothing make-
believe about me,"
she purrs, a feline
forepaw prodding
his crotch: "Watch."

6
A simple thong secures her sweep of hair
as an Amazon archer pauses to adjust
her deerskin vest left unattached
to allow ample movement for her breasts.
With care she measures twelve paces.
Enough! She draws her bow.
The arrow

(did we see or merely hear it?)
cleaves a heart-shaped piece of pine
in half.

The Serbian knife-thrower
melancholy and too drunk
to perform
rests his head against a post.
He's homesick and weeps with shame.
He wants to walk again in the woods with his son and
     daughter.

7
Skewered on a spit
above red-hot coals
a roasting goat.

Before any hint of rain
when the air thickens
it smells of horse
shit, fish, goats,
pigs, incense,
woodsmoke and wine:
a dense cloud that gathers
over walkways twisting
among the vendors' tents.

8
Step inside. Shadowy
lean-to stalls
ask for our souls—
What do we yearn to see?

 The Pope's young bride
is the pouting gypsy

girl who rode a pony
standing on her hands.

But the monkey-boy!
The horned giraffe!
A fire-eating Turk!
The fabulous Minotaur of Crete?

Under her flickering lamp
an onyx-eyed Veronese
crone casts fortunes
in the entrails of geese.

Couples gather armfuls of straw
into a corner the crowd
chooses to ignore;
in the unquiet dark
we ask no names
but shed costumes
and masks
to discover each other.

9
Distant thunder. The last revelers
wander off; sink
down in
inextricable passageways
together and alone.

Dawn brings its half-light
to the abandoned square.
Tents are unstaked,
rolled, taken up
as torches gutter out
and horses shake in their sleep

while upon us all
the early morning rain
promising
not pardon but mercy
murmurs its blessing.

Authority

More circumspect than hunters setting
traps in the tawny Tuscan hills,
clerics plotted their steps:
which witnesses required torture?
All the while accumulating
evidence for the Inquisitor's file.

Forsaking caution, Galileo
acknowledged each enemy
unnerved him. He grew brash,
contemptuous—the child
he'd been before the world
discovered him. True,
he'd sought preferment. Who
has not? No matter—he
was appalled by authority
unless it favored him. . .

Among faithful supporters
he counted three emissaries
to the Papal Court. Also
a prince. A Minister
of State, no less. And, yes,
the Grand Duke of Tuscany.

Behind bejeweled fingers
they grinned, they tittered,
to hear their friend—his cup
filled to spilling—propose
his toast to progress; then
pronounce the Pope, "A dupe,
a dullard, a simpleton.
A worm. A brass-brained dolt.

A sheep. A braying ass
spooked by its own shadow."

Clearly, he feared no man
now. No—not even
pious Pope Urban
who strangled songbirds
in the Vatican garden
when they disturbed him.

Galileo Speaks with God on a Midsummer Night of Shimmering Stars

1
The moon is late and still the hour shines.
Cedars shudder in their blackness.
From far off a faint jingling.
"Do you hear our tower bells?
The wind plays them like a timbrel."

2
Planets appear to glow with their own life.
The fabric of the heavens at any moment
might become a glimmering tapestry.
Truth—to an unquiet mind—is never quite enough.

3
"The stars blaze above us.
How did you know we would love them so?"

4
He wishes to ask a wicked question
but his courage fails him:
Why offer us such beauty—distant
bells tremulous in the high wind;
the diffident dance of the great trees;
this wonder that steals our breath away—
and certain death?

5
How long has he lived alone?
He believes he cannot know
how to cherish a woman
beyond his passion
for her; always

fearing she'll leave him.
The dread of an unwanted child.

6
"I understand my duty.
But you have formed a darkness so vast and lovely
it hurts my heart."

With the restless shuttling sound
of a spirited loom at work
the night wind turns the sky to silk.

The Death Of Galileo

1
His sentence—life imprisonment—is commuted
to house arrest. Confined to the hilltop
villa near his daughter's convent, he writes
until his sight fails him. Welcomes visits
from Milton. From Thomas Hobbes. One woman
weaves intelligence with her tender humor.
She reads to him and he adores her. Until
this moment no one has ever troubled him
with kindness. "*My* fault—who pets a wild pig?"

She answers him with laughter. Then gossip.
He loves it—always has—plucked ripe from court.

Blind, he paces a gabled room, halting
at the latched window which overlooks
a leafless orchard. Plodding down the path,
his favorite mule follows a fieldhand home.
He hears its bell clanging, clanging. So like
what? Venice? Yes, years ago. Early
morning. The call to the marketplace. Leaving
its chill, twilight ebbs from the windowpane.
He settles his bulk on the bed, gasping for breath.
Fingers pluck a horseblanket over his smock.

2
Though the age died when he was brought to trial,
upon his death his argument made its way
across Europe. Beyond guarded borders
it was whispered. Tested. The results sheltered
in private libraries. Advanced in learned societies.
And—this would not astonish him—in the secret
teachings of Jesuit fathers in China and Japan.

3
Will we learn too late to love? On one small
satellite of the sun the mind imagines
its origin: from interstellar clouds
of dust, solar wind, daylight, earth
itself struck by lightning, soothed by rain,
consciousness emerges. He brought us this
vision of the universe—a process ongoing,
accessible to the thought of man or woman.

In nature are we not bonded to one another?
Stars, atoms, grass, water, soil.
Doves that disturb the peace of the vineyard.
Two hawks circling a sleeping hill. In time
we learn that each question is a prayer—
will we learn to love each day without fear?
Already his plum orchard standing bare
in the dead of winter prepares its purple bloom
while dawn illuminates a silent room.

NIGHT'S BODY

It was full moon while I was down at Takaunga, and the beauty of the radiant, still night was so perfect that the heart bent under it. You slept with the doors open to the silver Sea. . . One night a row of Arab dhows came along, close to the coast, running noiselessly before the monsoon, a file of brown shadow-sails under the moon.

—Isak Dinesen

Painted Horses

Horses after first light browsed the border
of the plateau. The sun had burned away
a thin mist; earth gleamed. Birds circled, screeching.

Because of their wild grace how huge the horses
loomed in our eyes. How stern when they stalked us
through a fitful sleep. Finding them larger than life,

on cavern walls—temples of the imagination—
we painted them in proportion to their spirit:
Running wild, they'd nip or bite each other—

Sometimes in pleasure but often with malice.
They ran the way a full river flows, headlong,
assuming the shape of the land then swiftly

overwhelming it. Round-eyed, whinnying.
The fierce ones charging, blowing and frothing.
Fights were brief but furious. Kicking, chomping.

Or they reared, snorting, and pummeled with their hooves.
Today we excavate the battered bones;
the scarred hides are preserved in mudbanks, tar.

What do we know that is sacred? Water,
rocks. Without these the weather of each day
is insignificant, crags cast deep shadows

then withdraw them, they offer no shelter
to a troubled creature. Fire—we carried it
flickering from the mouths of caves. Down dark

hillsides, the steep terrain broken, footing
uncertain. Cautiously we crossed creeks; never

more than one torch upon the water. Or

more frequently followed the tumbling, coursing
water through gullies illuminated
only by wings of flame. Which we brought on,

wavering, flaring, into sunlit fields. Fowl
fled through the brush or flapped above it, striving,
desperate. Birds bewildered us. Their cries were ours,

but their flight, their songs, suggested another world.
Taking on their plumage and their piercing eyes,
the distant heavens settled among the trees.

Trees were worshiped, dreaded. What other life
joined beauty and necessity? Grass. Windswept swales
where the nimble-footed horses romped or grazed;

where mares cajoled their spindly foals to stand
tottering. Testing balance, vision, and nerve.
Learning attention. Alert then to the scent of smoke

thickening the air, throbbing under its dark warning,
all turned with one mind and raced across the green plateau
thirty thousand years before this morning.

Living Again

Then he remembered the blue house where they'd lived.
Her hair nesting on her shoulder as in this photo.
The firm weight of her breast. His hand opened.
The frame struck the floor; glass shattered—

He tore his shirt to reach the pain. Now
he choked on the silence in the cabin.
No breath. The door banged open. He stumbled

through the pines. Into the meadow. Pools of snow-
melt among the budding thistles, lupine.
Still he did not cry out. His mouth a mute O.

Above the silver river he saw a hawk flicker.
His chest on fire, he forgot his right hand
full of excuses. Fell among mule-ear. Grass

growing dim. Waking, on his hands and knees,
he noticed the pain that gripped his heart
had eased into his shoulders. Deep

in his belly his breath welled up. Again
the hawk flashed its blood-red tail
in the wind. He rose, slowly. Saw tawny

cattails nodding. Poppies. The first purple
thistles. He listened. For what? When
he was about to die he'd remembered the dark

rain in her voice. Spring rain falling all night
in the Sierra, lifting the river above its bank,
drenching the green meadow, waking sun-gold blossoms.

Then did his heart recover its rhythm, his mind
its balance? He took two steps. Heard water churn;
slosh sedge grass, slap rocks. A chill light

rushed downstream. When he saw it shiver past
the black mudbank already he'd begun to choose
this life in which our words follow one another
to the end: snowmelt, granite, hawk, poppies, river.

Warm Rain

Night and day the rain spills its silence
over us. South of Galilee not one hand
tends the orchards; the pipe-fed fields
idle on the floor of the Ghor
or *Al Gawr* absorb the dripping stillness.
Twelve days' rain drenches the valley.
High water in the wadis. Only
these girls wrapped in grey wool
each morning gather by the river.

Brooding sky. Gravel soil
swept away, water
roiling downstream,
splashing into the salt
slow sea. Green reeds
glowing. Two girls lean over

the bank. Laughing, they lower
their bare feet into the flow.

Together they unbundle
rolls of soiled clothes
to catch the current
flapping past. Upriver
the sky flashes silver—
A stand of slender young
willows washing
their hair in the high wind.

Under the rain the river
Jordan rises, trembling,
the lean brown arm
of the dead
god growing restless in the reeds.

When They Leave

When they leave the world will be at peace
forever. A room with wide windows
shut against the weather. Wind
beyond the glass bending the brilliant maples.
Will we hear wings beating out of those trees?

Who can inhabit the unholy sleep
of the soul once they wander
silently away? Who'll bark, howl,
bray, croak, whirr, whinny, all
together raise their joyful noise? None

of these creatures who breed and birth
their young and feed
so near to us
a man forgets
the grace granted to each one—

Cattle
because they are convenient—

Coyotes
because they are not—

The cats
which remind us of our debts—

The sentimental dog who swallows his pride
and happily prevails
by licking plates.

Ordinary horses
who carry their ancient hearts under ours.

Also the bristling hog we hate and eat.

The customary spotted goat we know
will never acknowledge its guilt--

Black clouds of crows who strut
among the muddy furrows
at seedtime. Hosts of locusts
floating like smoke over the fields—
The brown bats in love with our streetlamps.

Droves of animals who mate and thrive
and swarm before our eyes only
to disappear when we dream
because they are too innocent
to survive.

First Morning

The only autumn I have known
without my father is finished—
a flash storm, the worst since his death,
and last night's freeze: granite outcrop
wears a milky glaze. Lean hemlocks
stand sheathed in ice. At dawn walking
across the meadow to the woods
I wish for the warmth of his voice
once more. A peaceable man—only
injustice angered him. How might
we meet again if not hiking
in these frosted fields? No hunter,
he loved to discover animals
in their habitat and leave them
undisturbed. Which he thought just.
"They earn their peace among us.
Let them be." The wren in its nest;
the half dozen frogs surviving
--who can say how—in a bog-hole;
two owls attracted to the gloom
of the horse barn.
                    His patience will take
years to learn—it's time I start home
to my own children. Emerging
from a stand of pines shagged with ice
I surprise a fox and it bolts
to safety. Brushy tail barely
twitching the white grass, leaving no
trace. Drops of ice sparkle among
manzanita. Where my path ends
cold sunlight strikes a frozen sheen
on the county road. It's the first
morning of winter and the world
is made of glass the heart must break.

Trio

1

When Clara wrote that her husband had attempted suicide
(Schumann in robe and slippers bolted the house—
hurled himself into the frigid Rhine)
Brahms came at once to Bonn. He was twenty-one.
Could he be mistaken? He feared for Robert,
while Clara, mother of seven, quivered like a bride.
He was undone by his desire. And her distress.

He wanted to hold her to his breast,
knowing the embrace meant more than comfort.

2

Might he bow his boyish head before her grief
and kiss her hands? They were not delicate,
though she appeared to be. Agile, yet tender;
hands capable of toil or exquisite performance.

He murmured his farewell and fled for home.
It was early March—the night bright and cold.
Work alone might release him from his shame;
weren't these two—man and wife—his dearest friends?

3

In his study he drew the tattered drapes.
On the floor the pile of familiar manuscripts;
a glass, a solitary saucer. The room
of a single-minded man. His cigars,
twin candelabra, two music stands. Striving
to complete his Piano *Trio in B*,
he labored all night though the fire was down.

He sat then, silent. In the diminishing dark
he wished again to kiss her trembling hands.

The Kill

For three days the pack had trailed the great elk
herd through thin forest of pine and maple,
the wolves lean and limber in the mottled light
falling on their fur. Sunlight silvered it
but in the shade they were grey or grey-black,
and their trot was so effortless they seemed
to be dreaming. On the fourth morning the herd
fled into a meadow where the wolves attacked
an aging buck, snapping at his flanks and rump.
Once they'd dropped him they tore into his hide.

Their teeth ripped the buck open. Their breathing
grew labored; rasping, narrow chests heaving—
Long snouts dripping as they glutted on venison.

Feeding until dusk, they shared the carcass
with cawing ravens wafting up and down,
plucking bits of flesh then prancing away.

When they'd eaten all but the long shards of bone,
antlers, hooves, portions of the shredded hide,
the wolves cleansed themselves of the elk's dense scent.

They lapped at their fur, ruffled and bloodied.
They swabbed it with slobber then matted it
with their mouths, meticulously tonguing it.

Those that paired off went on bathing. Rising
through their fatigue they turned to lick the ears
or spine of a partner, another. Soon
their coats glowed like woodsmoke in the moonlight.
Retreating among the trees, the pack gathered
itself in a clearing. Trampling their tight
circle into the grass, the wolves lay down

in the peace of all that lives, all that dies,
all that's holy here. Then they shut their eyes
and slept with their hearts beating beneath the night.

The Half-Dark

At dusk when the wind falls the first thick flurries
brighten the air but it soon darkens.
The ticking sound of the snow
is the sound of time settling
on the tin roof of the newsstand
(its faulty lamp flickering on and off)
and over the traffic slowing, almost halting, in the street.

While the city sleeps it remembers snow
piled streetside in dusky banks. A wreath
of moonlight—the ice encrusted fountain.
The innumerable angles of legs tucked
behind each desk or climbing stairs
in the half-dark of the soul. Now
it dreams the blue buildings of our breath.

Eleven Sketches in Charcoal

*French trapper's drawings abandoned in an
Oglala camp on the Powder River, Wyoming
Territory, Winter 1866*

1
The four who stole the soldiers' horses drive them
into the wind without rest. Dawn to dusk.
A wolf wind, swift and sharp, biting their faces.
They ride without reins or bits or halters.

From the fort on the plateau clear to the river
swales of old snow glimmer
between patches of prairie grass speckled
and pale as a spring fawn.

2
      When the riders cross the river
      into camp the ice under-
      foot (black, opaque)
      never quakes. It
      rings hard as iron.

3
Their wives, turning four ways, chant their names
over blankets, knives, a bone-handled hatchet.
A bonfire blazes—

(The geometric beadwork of their dresses.)

4
The trader's coffee and heavy kettles.
His free-hand map of the river
to this point. Unadorned
the rawhide bag that preserves his sketches.

5
Dogs slather a girl's hand for scraps.

6
        In the lodge hides hang
        beside ornamental skulls,
        distended claws, strips
        of dried meat. Quivers
        bristling arrows. Below
        on the beaten floor
        spears, stone clubs.
        The haft of an axe.

7
        Swathed in a remnant of
        buffalo robe a stack
        of no more than four
        single-shot rifles.

                        To one side the word
                        effroi appears:
                        Fright? Or dread?

8
Children chase their voices through the cottonwoods.
What calls them back?
Flutes. Whistles. Pulsing drums.
All night dancers, shuffling, circle the flames.

9
Couples, seated, wrap themselves in shadows.
Darting among the dancers
with her armful of broken boughs
grandmother feeds the fire—
Sparks leap and laugh. A bright cold night.

10
Warriors enter the ring—a few
rapid strokes. Markings
imprecise. For the hour
thickens now with smoke
as the throng whirls and
the hand surrenders its will
in one irregular scrawl:
Je suis pris de terreur.

11.
No signature but beside this final scene
effroi is repeated.
In haste—smeared.

Thin indolent cattle crowd
close for warmth. Mules
edge among them. Left
alone the horses steam in the dark.

Winter Night

Moonlight—fresh snow fills the meadow—
the blizzard that buried the road
beyond the storm-fence has blown off.
No wind lifting skittish clouds of
powder. No tracks but ours. Only
the owl's shadow gliding over
Alder Creek. Through the trees we see
the work winter does, the snowfield
glittering, widening, using
up all the spare white light the way
a river stretches in the sun. . .
Suddenly the sheen of this ice-
sharp wind that brings tears to your eyes.
Our voices, while we hike downhill,
construct a life more plausible
than the words that glow before us,
then dissolve in the dark.
                              Until
we find the young fox the owl gorged
itself on. Blood and bone. Kneeling,
we cover it with shallow snow
dogs will dig tomorrow.
                              Silence
thrives in the black night and we know
at the heart of this clarity
is sorrow. This is what I want
to understand as we turn home
beneath the stars, their fervent fire:
How solitude survives us. When
I reach for your hand you offer
it and we touch without speech, we
embrace. Then stand here together
in this moment, this white meadow,
which takes our breath away and fills

us with wonder. The cold world so
still its beauty shines regardless
of the cub's blood, the drifted road.

Chiaroscuro

In autumn when seagulls went winging over the Seine
and the implacable plane trees were turning yellow
she chose to sketch them in charcoal. Under shivering
chestnut trees on the Champs-Élysées she studied
three leaves spattered on the pavement. Pausing
on her familiar route to the Rodin museum,
beside a brick wall she bent to photograph
the spikey fruit fallen onto the damp stones
at her feet. For a later day. Rising, she saw
drizzle gleaming on mansard rooftops, a host
of swallows flocking home. The weather turned her
toward her upstairs flat overlooking the Metro
and the market where she bought her tin of tea.

Also, for her stewpot, the blushing pink pig's
head collared with a wreath of flowers. Pointedly
she set down her sketchpad and raised a window
to await the evening. Long ago she'd learned
how a line in darkness differs from a line in light:

How each form acquires its depth with a certain
loss of identity. As dusk arrives freighted
with threats and promises, rumbling through the city.

A train besmirched by smoke, steam. Doors clatter
open, passengers abandon the day's journey,
crowding the platform. No longer would she draw
trains leaving behind their twin silver tracks
in echoes of light and shadow, knowing the more
a line repeats itself the less it grows.

While she watched a young woman struggle
to unfurl her umbrella streetlights sputtered on.

Beneath the staircase to the elevated train
a man in a coal-dark vest sat strumming
Granada. Then Villa-Lobos. Sor. Debussy.
Standing before her window drinking black
tea laced with honey, she asked herself
if what we wish is the soul of what we are—
Now she was neither working nor finished working
she became, as she wished, one with the shadows,
listening to the sonorous rain of the guitar.

The Sea

It is a human sharing in the rhythm of the sea
and the moon
and animal breeding
and the stars.
—Ernesto Cardenal, *Love*

Helpless her hands lose hold, slip away.
As though night hides an undertow
which lifts her warm weight on its arm.
Along the dark she drifts
out of sight—
A solid sea-wall divides the surf
from the shore splashed with rocks.

When the man wades out to find her
the moon pulls up its anchor.
It slides free of the tide—
The hull of his soul sails on
the sky, his body is a buoy
in the black seams of the waves.
A drunken crew dances on the deck.

In sleep we float far apart. Voyage
in different dreams that wreck
in the wind. And fear
death in the deep bed. Then swim
toward land. Birdsong. The blue scent
of wild lilac. Suddenly here we stand
on the stones of consciousness, shining, short of breath—

Homage to Anna Akhmatova

1
We have murdered time but it will rise
in judgment of our acts, she believes;
this is the resurrection we await—
Her first husband had been arrested
by Lenin's *Cheka*. Without trial
he was stood against a wall and shot.
Buried with countless others in a pit.
Now, though their son Lev is innocent
of any crime, for eighteen years
he's held in prison to silence her.
Interrogated, beaten, isolated,
sentenced to hard labor. Finally
condemned to die like his father
should she fail to cooperate
with the state... In the prison yard
every morning a firing squad
assembles. Rope, sidearms, rifles.

2
Immediately after Stalin orders
her books confiscated, destroyed,
a dozen solitary men and women
recite her lines to preserve them,
invisible. Hurriedly she gathers
her papers (notebooks, diary, letters);
all that haven't been seized she burns
in her flat.
       Night and day fearing
for another's life—it's her son's;
it might be yours or anyone's—
Anna is compliant. Or she
appears to be. As with her slow
long-legged stride she navigates

the gloom of a northern night, smoke
driven to ground by the drenching
rain. No light at the corner. She
gropes for the stairs. A doorlatch slips.

3
Tall and gaunt, she stoops to enter.
The tasseled lamp reveals her eyes,
pale, austere; its shadows sharpen
her angular Old Believer's face.
Lord, this sudden fire! Her heart.
One moment for the pain to lapse.
The brief embrace before her host
offers a taste of pastry. Tea. Then
with a quavering in her throat
she delivers from memory
her guest's unforgiving poetry,
as clear as water and as necessary:

"I, half-mad, mourning the past. . .
the black whisper of misfortune. . .
I am forbidden to appear anywhere."

Anna, her head tilted back, listens
to the fearful tremolo in her friend's
voice: "Blood smells only like blood...
And if they gag my exhausted mouth. . .
time will rise like a corpse."
                                    In return
she, in a low melodious tone,
recites her beloved Pushkin. Blok.
Tsvetayeva—dazzling, distraught—
and Osip Mandelstam: "Ten steps
away no one hears our speeches."
This, Anna prays, is true. Rising
to leave, she retrieves her shawl.

4
Just shy of the doorstep she searches
the sulphurous murk, discerning
that pair near the stairwell. Wet, chilled,
the two agents stalking her lurk
beneath a neighbor's windowshade,
drinking under broad umbrellas,
stamping their boots for warmth. So
Lev lives still! Still the terror. Each
night they shadow her with such disdain
they dare her to discover them. While
in her soul reverberates the threat
she knows by heart: *Should you persist
in writing poems, or publish. . .If
you protest his sentence; confer
with foreign authors or complain
to treacherous reporters. . .* Will
they trail her home? No sign of her
alarm. With that deliberate
dignity of one who fears your pain
and imminent death more than her own,
she descends the stairs. At her feet
the dark street shivers in the rain.

The Dance

While lanterns lolled above the sweet spring grass
fresh-mowed for the party—gleams of light
lilting like a dance of bees among the boughs—
we lay in the orchard. And drank little wine
because the fragrance of your auburn hair
was all I knew of longing. I spoke your name
with the darkness in my throat and you whispered
mine more clearly than I'd ever heard it
uttered. Or hoped to. The delicate tongues
of leaves in the mouth of the sky. The night
wind warm, yes, and your skirt fell from your knees.
But voices climbed the hill. Your father called
a reel. Two fiddles sang while couples clapped.

Memory spares us nothing touched by love—
You wept without a sound while my fingers brushed
your blouse—apple blossoms—then we walked down
among the last trees, their shifting shadows,
into the light to join the others. Pairs
twirling, taking hold, in time releasing.
Women whirling their wide skirts over
all the lawn. Men young and old unwilling
to shed their fine coats, sweating with pleasure.
Yet they stopped to stare at your tears. Tell me
tonight what's more dear than your hand in mine
and that proud toss of your hair? All these years.

The Deer Come Down

1
It is summer. Our sixth year of drought. The deer come down
from the parched mountain meadow pale as a hayfield,
the mule-ear cropped, manzanita plucked bare,
lupine wilting in an empty wind.

The last snow gleams on a granite slope where the sun flashes.

A fallen pine shredded by beetles disgorges its red scent.
Out of habit the herd tries the spring rainpool—
It is baked, chalky, the fringe of sawgrass rasping.
After they forage on pennyroyal
like our souls they come down from the dry heights
seeking water. They risk free-fall
on that steep grade to follow their thirst
through a stand of brittle pines.
Eyes dark and clear
with one desire.
Is this all? Or
what dread wisdom guides them
so far downstream
outflanking the fishing camp,
the silted well,
the emigrant girl's gravestone furred by moss?

Heedless of human intention—they have never known
regret—the deer ignore the dog yawping,
straining its chain. The gun
gleaming in the corner of the poacher's cabin.

2
You signal silence, your finger touches your lips—
A doe halts in the dusty clearing. Spindly,
delicate, she dares us to approach.

Moist eyes search the mottled woods.

Finding two truant fawns, she turns, trots off.
They amble after her. While we watch the herd
emerge from the shadows of the trees
the sun pours down on Mill Creek.
It plunges into the current, leaping,
sliding, glistening. How gently
their shoulders slope over the bank,
their precarious balance undisturbed
by the dog. The poacher's tracks. Or our scent.

Wholly alert, they no longer tremble. They bow their heads
in praise of the present moment streaming with light
as if it were eternal, and it is, and they drink
for once without haste or fear.
Yes, this is the other world—
When we die we come here.

Looking at the Man

1
Looking at the man who hangs on the tree
stripped bare, black

hair swirled with sweat
as if he had been running away

from his youth to climb
the spine of this hill

at noon while the heavens howl
then shut with a hush

to seal the sun in the tomb
of a winter night,

nine birds like leaves
that loop the hard hilltop
witness such weather.

2
Looking at the man and at his mother

hunching herself the way women wait
in a downpour, watching

clouds cleave apart for the moment
no one doubts he's going to die

now that every song but pain is gone
from his eyes, his limbs

slack like a hawk nailed
by one brown wing to the barn door

finally falling limp, crying out
when the lust in his eyes grows dim

we are moved to believe
the blue skull
of the sky hears him.

Now

1

When we lived in deep dusk the mind of man or woman
was a night-blooming flower. The bulbs
were buried in the black earth. Now we begin
to remember the story of everlasting night:
When we dream and desire no redemption.
The elemental pull of the moon
over the pearl-seeded sea
of our souls. Night of unknowing
that shelters the golden bees,
poppies, a slim green snake.
Awake in the fragrant dark we taste
its salt on our lips when we kiss.

2

Forgive us—in a brief and busy history
blood draped the chambers inside each skull,
the walls of the mind were crimson.
The blood we spilled every day flowed into the fabric
of our lives, the bright flag of our belief.
We invented Europe and original sin and absolution.
We invented witchcraft, heresy, and the balance of power.
We determined the mind of man
must rule the body of the earth
where we record the millisecond of each missile-launch.
We calculate a diminished response time.
We acknowledge our margin for error.

3

We remain uncertain of the morning
when the apple orchard flowers.
The sun of midsummer ripens and falls
and deer slip down from the high meadows.
Bells ring across the valley. Walking home

from school our children ask why do we die?
At dusk a steep snow quiets the foothills.
Earth glows in winter light.
The luster of a pearl—
the moon rising
in the night
sky.

Tree House

1
All morning with my wife I labored
over that house, then left it
for our children
to devise the door. Left them, too,
the rope ladder. Still its spiral rungs
like stigmata burn
the pattern of their purpose in our flesh.

Together on the porch we take our rest—
We climbed so long
in and out of that tree
my arch bears the ache of each branch
underfoot. Unable effortlessly
to open, my palm remembers the grip
of those limbs, the hammer, the rope.

2
Like trout our children float in the shadows
of forked boughs. In the bare-bones house
built of baling wire, weathered wood, leafy roof,
nothing more substantial than their dread
of falling hard to the earth forms
their floor. They hide their faces. Headfirst
they emerge, they splatter paint on the door!
They cry—first fright, then joy!
Leaves glow with glee,
feet and hands learn the boles
that bear weight. Up and down
the trunk and leaping
branches, laughter crawls
across the cool afternoon.

3
Shadows flood the grass and sink
the odd artifacts
of our hours: hammer, handsaw, paint-
brush stained blood
red. Ruler, pliers. Paper
plates, plastic cups. The bucket
of chicken bones plucked clean at supper.

Forgotten too when they sleep is the rope
coiled neat as a molecule within
night's body, every rung
imprinted in us now.
Overhead a tree whirls
across the sky. A tree of stars
where our children stir and dream

they are flying from limb to limb
among the shining creatures taking shape
the moment the mind makes them out—
The Hunter, two Bears, the Princess, the Swan,
dance on the dark floor of heaven.
Dance like the light that leaps in our eyes
when our children climb down from the tree at dawn.

Raccoons

First the thick woods above the river—
Then nightfall as the road plunges
through wide farmland and the wind smells so fresh
I imagine cornflowers nodding in the fields.
No, it's the new-mown grass—
An electric fence flanks the artillery range
where the prairie is cropped short to discourage fires.
Tonight the barracks are too warm for blankets;
the troops twist in their sleep.
                              Wind sweet as grass
bathes the tanks, somber in their stillness.
And huge howitzers and the half-dozen mortars in place
for morning maneuvers. I drive faster, unswerving.
Then, suddenly, slow. . . Just ahead they shine. . .

A low chain bobbing beside the road. I can't see
what joins them until they stop, struck blind
by my oncoming lights—
Seven in all return from their raid
of the garbage bins behind the mess hall.
Mother with your young
fed now, heading home,
to meet the danger in our eyes
you cover yours with that black mask:

You know the death in our hands, in our speeding cars.
The dream in the turret of the starlit tank.
The sleep in the cool throat of the cannon
while the arc of the mortar shell grows more precise
than men or women, game birds, the stray cub crossing the
road.

Mother of the low-bending, sure-footed night,
with your belly slung above the earth

you assert your body between the bones
of six plump cubs and the steel and chrome
rattling toward you. Driving on
under the green wind and the stars burning
above the fields, close-cut, prepared for war,
I pray to you
not for your life but for mine
as we pass—
Your brood behind you, bellies full,
trotting down the road through the black-eyed night.

Nighthawk

1
I love this storm—you do, too—its flash and glimmer!
Lost Child Creek rises, roiled by rain, the overflow
seeping under the red rocks in the meadow,
swelling the white roots of the weeds.

Lightning scars the dark sky behind the pines.
We run through the thicket—
rain sweeps the clearing.

"I can't go home. Hold me."
"Are you crying?"
"Hold me."

2
Who can sleep?
This gentle, insistent
rain all night
saying your name.

3
The morning gleams with wet
light as we walk the meadow
where you discover blue
larkspur. Wild iris.

Encompassed by the marsh
marigolds, fawn lilies,
spindly stickweed, a rain-
pool ripples the sun.

It shakes itself, shining.

4
"I'm not like this. I'm not!"

5
After you leave
the leaning aspen
shimmer in the water.

6
White-tail deer browse for berries until twilight
draws them down to the lake. They disappear
into dusk. Above the trees a nighthawk
revolves around its solitary cry.

A tune too shrill for joy—
Peeent-peent. Peent-peent.
What does it seek in the deep sky?

What does it hope to find
on the darkening earth?
The first stars burnish the lake
and silence falls like a black wind.

Summer Night

In the dark a loud spattering that streaks
our windows. A hush. A downpour. Water
probes slack gutters and uncertain shingles.
The rain is blind but it finds what it seeks.
Along the arching limbs of an elm it searches,
then plummets into meticulously weeded beds
where pools gather, bubbling in the black loam.

A torrent now that wakes all the flowers:
Big blowsy roses, glossy azaleas.
And the bold, fragrant, half-mad gardenia
that loves attention and never blushes.

The house grows cool; shivers. After the whine
of a car—at this hour—on the wet street,
I listen to your breathing beside me.
Darkness and rain. In our corner room late
at night we lie together and won't sleep
because the soul longs for darkness and rain.

Enjoy the Land

1
A sudden shower soaks the granite slope.
The sky clears, the moonlit grasses glisten,
already the runoff tumbles splashing
into Deer Creek. I'll cross it four or five
times walking downstream. Water cascading
over rocks, rushing beneath the aspen
and oak that shelter the foothills, spilling
from skeletal ancient flumes, then, slowly,
chuffing through a network of flood channels,
greening the valley. Tireless as the blood
that sustains love and braves any distance.
Or why does a man seek the solitude
that troubles him?
      In the dripping shining
quiet I miss my son in Nebraska
and my two daughters in California.
Here a full moon illuminates the old
tribal burial ground. Long neglected,
it's overgrown. The thicket opens
where summer herds—mule deer and blacktails—
at dusk travel tenacious zigzag trails
into an upland meadow. Which they share
with coyotes, squirrels, jays, vultures. "Enjoy
the land," Thoreau wrote, "but own it not."

2
I haven't learned to let go. May never learn
to live without the hope that haunts parents,
the weight of our regret. I pick my way
through outcrop and thistles onto a path
worn by campers, hikers. Hearing the wind
riffle the wild pasture.
      A bull's skull

ringed by lupine holds its cupful of snow—
white rainwater, a lambent light, the moon
more at home in the meadow than I am—
Long after his children are grown a man
still carries his family in his heart.
Turning back, I follow the footpath down
through rippling grass. With luck I'll arrive
after dawn: the sun like a seed sprouting
from the hayfield and the almond orchard,
the roadside patch of vetch. Daylight blooming
beside the black road into town. Always
we long for those we've loved in the silence
of what was whispered, wept, or left unsaid.
Now because we bear them with us—welcome
companions—each of us is more than one
man or woman. A city of souls, we greet
the morning among the living and the dead.

Acknowledgments

The author gratefully acknowledges the editors and publishers of the books and chapbooks in which these poems have appeared: *The Donner Party*, George Braziller, Inc. (1972, 1989, & 2012), published simultaneously by Doubleday Canada (1972); *Song in a Strange Land*, George Braziller, Inc., published simultaneously by Doubleday Canada (1974); *Scenes From Childhood*, Futharc Press (1987); *The Burning Bear*, Heatherstone Press (1991); *Earth's Eye*, Story Line Press (1994); *The Starry Messenger*, University of Pittsburgh Press (2003); and *Night's Body*, Turning Point (2011). Thanks are due, also, to the editors of publications in which poems selected for *Life and the Fields* were originally published or have been reprinted, including, among others: *American Poetry Review*, *The Antioch Review*, *Colorado Review*, *Harper's Magazine*, *The Iowa Review*, *The Kenyon Review*, *The Literary Review*, *The Massachusetts Review*, *New Letters*, *The New York Times*, *the new renaissance*, *The North American Review*, *The Sewanee Review*, *Volt*, and *The Yale Review*.

Thanks also to the Western Heritage Center for the Wrangler Award for *The Donner Party*, the Poetry Society of America for the Alice Fay di Castagnola Award for *Song in a Strange Land*, and *The Sewanee Review* for the Allen Tate Prize for Poetry, awarded for six poems in *The Starry Messenger*.

Among the new and uncollected poems, "Iron, Old Tin, & Wood" originally appeared in *Elkhorn Review*. "A Valley Oak in Early Spring" and "Early Morning in November" have been published in *Redwood Coast Review*. "Lines at 2 a.m. on the Sea of Cortez," "In Wind and Rain," and "The Angel of

Solitude" were first published in *The Sewanee Review*. "Building a Fire" first appeared *in Poetry Flash*.

Made in the USA
San Bernardino, CA
05 December 2018